Troubleshooting
the
Troubleshooting
Course

or Debug d'Bugs

Robert F. Mager

Pitman Management and Training
a division of
PITMAN LEARNING, INC.
Belmont, California

Editorial director: Joan Wolfgang
Text and cover designer: Susan True
Illustrator: Duane Bibby
Production manager: Patricia Clappison
Manufacturing manager: Susan Fox

ISBN-0-8224-9370-5
Library of Congress Catalog Card Number: 82-81980
Printed in the United States of America.
1.9 8 7 6 5 4 3 2 1

Contents

But First...

Once upon a time in the land of Bugadoo, Thumbs Turkey gathered up his blunderbuss and headed out.

"Where are you going?" asked his neighbor.

"I'm going out to shoot me some terrible Troubles," replied Thumbs and headed straight for the woods. Before long he chanced upon a Trouble sunning on a rock.

"Hello, there," greeted the Trouble. "Where are you headed?"

"I'm headed out to shoot me some Troubles," replied Thumbs. "That'll fix 'em."

"Oh," said the Trouble. "And how will you know when you see one?"

"Why, I'm told they look a lot like Bugs, you know," snipped Thumbs and went merrily on his way. Some time later he came upon a Trouble prancing through a meadow.

"Hello there," jollied the Trouble. "Where are you headed?"

"I'm headed out to shoot me some Troubles," replied Thumbs. "That'll fix 'em."

"Oh," said the Trouble. "And how will you know one when you see one?"

"Well, they're pretty sneaky, you know," confided Thumbs and went merrily on his way. A long time later he burst upon a naked Trouble splashing in a pond.

"Hello there," hailed the Trouble. "Where are you headed?"

"I'm headed out to shoot me some Troubles," said Thumbs, brandishing his Mark III Troubleshooter. "That'll fix 'em."

"Oh," said the Trouble. "And how will you know one when you see one?"

"Well, you just have to know where to look," huffed Thumbs and went merrily on his way. And went ... and went ... and went ... until one day his Troubleshooter rusted clear through and its buss fell off ... leaving this Turkey with nothing but a Mark III Blunder.

And the moral of this fable is ... you can't fix 'em if you can't find 'em.

WHAT THE BOOK'S ABOUT

Things break, get out of adjustment, or just wear out, but preventive maintenance will keep most equipment working longer. Troubleshooting and repair will restore it to use when things go wrong. What is true of equipment is also true of instruction. It fails, gets out of adjustment, or becomes obsolete. Preventive maintenance will keep it working longer; troubleshooting and repair will restore it to usefulness when something gets out of whack.

This book is about how to detect differences between what IS and what OUGHT TO BE taught in courses designed to teach equipment maintenance. It is about how to detect errors in instructional content (WHAT is taught) and instructional practice (HOW it is taught). It won't show you how to spot all the errors ... just those that are costly, either because they bloat the instruction or they produce less effective troubleshooters than they might.

In short, this is a book about how to detect and clear common troubles from troubleshooting courses.

WHAT IT'S NOT ABOUT

The training of competent troubleshooters is only one factor that influences the efficiency and success of the maintenance operation. Other factors, such as policies on spares, reporting, trouble escalation (referring a trouble to the next level), and assignment of maintenance responsibilities, also influence the efficiency with which equipment is returned to service and kept running. But this book is not about these other factors.

It is not about the management of maintenance staffs, the care and feeding of customer engineering staffs, or such issues as levels or echelons of maintenance. Nor is it about how to conduct a complete course analysis or how to recognize problems that may or may not be attributable to instruction. All these are important, but they are not the present concern.

WHO IT'S FOR

It is for experienced troubleshooters who are either teaching or preparing to teach the maintenance of one or more pieces of equipment. It is also for their immediate supervisors. In addition, analysts, designers, and developers of maintenance instruction may well find the content useful as a basis for reviewing their own activities.

If you have had an instructor training course, so much the better. If it was recently, then you probably know a good deal about modern instruction, and Part III of this book will be useful to you mainly as a review. If your instructor training goes back farther than a couple of years, however, or if it was confined mainly to platform lecturing technique, you may need some brushup. There have been advances in the craft of instruction just as there have been in the design of hardware.

THE PLOT

There are three major components to any troubleshooting course: (1) the troubleshooting strategy to be taught, (2) course content, and (3) instructional practices and procedures. Since each component is likely to contain one or more common troubles, the plot of this book is to provide you with the tools you need to spot those troubles.

- Part 1 shows you how to derive a flowchart showing the ideal troubleshooting strategy for the equipment you are or will be teaching.
- Part 2 helps you to generate a list of the specific skills that anyone would need in order to put that troubleshooting strategy into practice. It also shows you how to build a chart that relates those skills to one another. This chart, called a skill hierarchy, will let you check whether all necessary skills are being taught and are being taught in a productive order.
- Part 3 helps you to check instructional practices and procedures. By presenting the key characteristics of the instructional state of the art along with a description of a model troubleshooting course in operation, it will help you to identify the major differences between actual and desirable instructional practices.
- Part 4 describes the common troubles found in troubleshooting courses and provides you with a checklist to focus your observations while reviewing (troubleshooting) such courses.

BUT FIRST...

Before diving into Part I, it might be helpful for you to glance over the questions on the Troubleshooting Checklist in Chapter 9. Although you will know how to apply each of the questions by the time you finish the book, a glance at them now may help you to focus your reading of Chapters 1–3.

PART ◇ 1

Troubleshooting Strategy

The status quo
Should best be bought
When things that are
Are things that ought.

1

The Anatomy of Troubleshooting
(Odds, Bodkin, Odds)

"Well, that might work for *you*, but *my* situation is *different!*"

How many hundreds of times have you heard that conviction expressed in one way or another? It's a common cliché, uttered mostly by people who confuse *strategy* (a general approach or plan of attack) with *tactics* (the specific steps for implementing the strategy). So when confronted with a new strategy, these people see only the detailed steps they would have to use to implement it. And since such tactics change from one situation and environment to another, these people quickly tell you that the tactics appropriate to your situation would not apply to their own. Then they leap to the conclusion that the strategy itself is useless to them.

Such illogic applied to your troubleshooting strategy lets them conclude that whatever *you* do when troubleshooting doesn't apply to *them* because *their* equipment is different. They can't see the usefulness of your strategy because they are blinded by your tactics. They can't see that your *principles* are sound because your specific steps don't apply to troubleshooting *their* equipment.

Fortunately, however, "them" is not you. You know perfectly well that efficient troubleshooting strategy is similar for all equipment, regardless of size, function, or purpose. You know that when equipment malfunctions, basic strategy requires you to identify and verify symptoms, locate the trouble, and then clear it. You know that, regardless of the equipment, if you *already* know where the trouble is, you start right in clearing it; and if you *don't* know where the trouble is, you take steps to locate it. And you know that the same is true whether you are troubleshooting the kitchen toaster or a giant blattmobile. The details (tactics) differ, but the approach (strategy) is the same.

Strategy is what this chapter is about. It explores the proposition that some troubleshooting strategies are considerably more productive than others and then presents the one that will get you from symptom to trouble with the least amount of time and effort. Using a flowchart picture of that strategy, you will derive the specific steps (tactics) for applying that strategy to your own equipment. Then you will be able to compare the ideal strategy with what is being taught and spot common troubles, if any, in your courses.

Trouble — now there's a word to look at more closely. In the equipment troubleshooting context, the word *trouble* implies that something has gone wrong and that that something is preventing the equipment from working *as well as it used to*. When troubleshooters locate the trouble they *fix* it — that is, they put the equipment *back* into working order.

But a troubleshooting course *may never* have been in working order before a problem is spotted, or it may have been working only fairly well. Moreover, it is highly unlikely that a single "fix"; that is, a single change in course practice, will put it into "normal operation." So, in the *course troubleshooting* context, it is more realistic to define *trouble* as an "opportunity for improvement." Whereas one or two remedies will often fix a machine, a dozen or more improvements are often required to fix a course.

TROUBLESHOOTERS ARE A SNOOPY LOT

Strange how quickly times change. Right now they are changing so fast that even our dictionaries can't keep up. Our garden-variety dictionary says that a troubleshooter is a person "who locates and repairs mechanical breakdowns." Our pompous dictionary says it is "an expert in discovering and eliminating the cause of trouble in mechanical equipment, power lines, etc."

Not bad, but far too narrow. Those may have been accurate definitions in the days before electronics and computers, but they are way out of date now. These days troubleshooters include all the people who are involved with locating and clearing troubles from all kinds of equipment, mechanical or otherwise. And with all the electrical and electronic equipment around, there sure is a lot of otherwise. Some people even think of physicians and psychiatrists as troubleshooters because they work to locate and clear physical and mental malfunctions. The locating part of the process is called *diagnosis*, and the clearing part is called *treatment* or *intervention*.

A troubleshooter, then, is someone who (a) hunts for or locates causes of malfunctions and (b) acts to eliminate or clear them. But being an experienced troubleshooter, you already knew that. What may have slipped your mind is the distinction between *locating* and *clearing*, a distinction that can make a large difference to both the cost of training and the efficiency with which troubleshooting is carried out on the job. The trouble locator needs diagnostic skills; the trouble clearer does not. The trouble locator often needs to know a great deal about how the equipment works; the trouble clearer doesn't need to know as much. Although these activities often overlap, they are different enough so that each function could be assigned to a different person. That is what happens when the *hotshot* troubleshooter is called in on those difficult problems. The hotshot is almost always called in just to locate a difficult trouble. Once the trouble is found, the local troubleshooters, or even the operators, are able to clear it.

With that distinction in mind, let's zero in on the nature of trouble locating.

ODD, ISN'T IT?

Know what troubleshooters are trying to do when they attempt to locate a trouble? They're trying to change the *odds*. If they have *no idea* where the trouble is when they begin, then from their point of view, odds are that the trouble could be any-where: there is equal probability that the trouble could be in any part of the equipment. If they come up with a *good idea* about where the trouble is, then the odds are no longer equal. There is a higher probability that the trouble is here rather than there. If they *know* where the trouble is, odds have been replaced by *certainty*. And that is the object of trouble-shooting — to move from a condition of no idea or some idea of where the trouble is to certainty about where the trouble is.

When troubleshooters *know* where the trouble is, they engage in clearing actions. They act to remove the malfunc-tion, usually by adjusting something or replacing something.

If they *don't know* where the trouble is, they need to engage in actions that will change their understanding from "I don't have any idea of where the trouble is" (equal probabili-ty) to "I think it's in this section of the equipment" (high probability) to "This is it" (certainty). Thus, the process of troubleshooting is the process of replacing probability with certainty.

THE TROUBLESHOOTING PURPOSE

Now hold on a minute. I'm not about to insult your experience by pretending you don't know that the purpose of trou-bleshooting is to locate and clear troubles. Besides, we've just discussed that. But we should spend a minute or so reviewing the larger purpose of troubleshooting, the purpose that is larger than the equipment itself: *to return the customer's equipment to operational status as fast as possible*.

The larger purpose is to maximize UP time and minimize DOWN time. "UP the equipment" is our motto.* It is not the purpose to follow some prescribed procedure, or to demonstrate one's dexterity at fine adjustments, or to prove one's eloquent grasp of theory. The purpose is to get the equipment UP and back in service fast, in a way that will keep it in service.

That may seem obvious, and it is obvious to troubleshooters in the field. But a strange thing seems to happen when these competent troubleshooters enter the classroom as instructors. The molecules in their heads get disarranged with peculiar, and sometimes costly, consequences. They suddenly seem to get all goggle-eyed about a thing called "theory," start talking about how their job is to "teach people how to think," and in general appear to forget everything they know about how to clear troubles *fast*. They sometimes don't teach the tricks they learned in the field, sometimes they deliberately refrain from teaching shortcuts, and some don't even tell their students about the *common* troubles they will encounter when *they* hit the field. It's as though they were embarrassed to teach in school the things they would surely teach on the job ... almost as though school is for theory and the job is for practice. It would be unfair to put any blame on instructors, though, when they haven't had training in the craft of instruction.

So while it may seem obvious that the larger purpose of troubleshooting is to get the equipment UP and back in service as soon as possible, you would never guess that by looking in on some troubleshooting courses. Rarely is the primary pur-

---

*No doubt you've noticed that the perfect subtitle for this book is "UP Your Course!" When the editor first saw that on the manuscript, though, she said, "NO WAY!" Oh, well. Since purring editors are easier to work with, I changed it.

pose of troubleshooting made crystal clear to course developers and instructors by management. Rarely do all these troubleshooting trainers understand that purpose in the same way, and design instructional content and practice to support that purpose. More common are those courses with instructors who pursue their own varying notions about ultimate purpose. Often instructional practices are observed that appear to be designed more for the convenience of course administration — lecture-in-the-morning, lab-in-the-afternoon — than for efficient accomplishment of the mission.

It is for this reason that you must place the larger purpose of troubleshooting in the front of your mind. It will keep you on track and ready to spot discrepancies between what IS and OUGHT TO BE taught in the way of troubleshooting strategy.

If you are an experienced troubleshooter, you know that down time is influenced not only by your troubleshooting skill, but by a number of other factors, such as the kind of spares you are allowed to keep handy. If you are allowed to stock only itty-bitty components instead of assemblies and subassemblies, you will *have* to troubleshoot to the component level even though that makes for longer down time.

Some companies prefer to stock only components because it reduces the cost of parts inventory (and makes the computer happy). These companies may praise the parts department for holding costs down and at the same time tear their hair out over the high cost of down time . . . without ever realizing that the former is the cause of the latter.

The object of troubleshooting is to UP the equipment by minimizing down time, sure. But accomplishment of that goal requires more than just competent troubleshooters; it requires an inventory policy that balances cost of spares against cost of down time.

INFO, INFO EVERYWHERE

Troubleshooters move from a state of *don't know* or *not sure* to *certain* about trouble location by collecting information. They collect symptoms. They interpret waveforms, read gauges and meters, smell, taste, and make substitutions. All their actions are intended to serve one purpose . . . *information collection*. And when they have collected enough to tell them where the trouble is, they *stop* and begin clearing the trouble. It is not only an inefficient use of time to keep on collecting information after the trouble location has been verified, it's sort of silly.

Remembering that the larger purpose of troubleshooting is to get that equipment UP and running as fast as possible implies something else about collecting information. It implies that the troubleshooter should go to the most potent source of information first, to the source that will provide the most information for the least amount of effort and time. Here are the six information sources typically available to the troubleshooter, listed roughly in order from most to least productive or time efficient.

1. Experience

The troubleshooter's memory is a key source of information about trouble location. Regardless of whether such memory was developed through hard knocks in the field or through careful instruction, it is a potent ally. A troubleshooter who knows from experience where the trouble is, or is highly likely to be when observing a particular set of symptoms, is able to bypass almost the entire information-collecting process. (It is always prudent, however, to verify symptoms.) If the troubleshooter already has the information, it would obviously be foolish not to go straight to trouble-clearing actions.

2. Operators

Imagine this dialogue between a detective and a judge.

Detective: ... and so I sent the witnesses away.

Judge: You what?

Detective: I sent the witnesses on their way.

Judge: And just why did you do that?

Detective: Because I'm a detective.

Judge: So?

Detective: If I let witnesses tell me who's guilty, I'd never get to detect.

Yes, of course it's silly. But it is no sillier than troubleshooters who avoid talking to operators because they think it demeans them to collect information from a source other than the hardware itself. Operators are often there when the troubles occur and can provide eyewitness accounts of great help, even sometimes pointing to the actual trouble spot itself. Of course, eyewitnesses are sometimes wrong, and they don't always provide useful information. But operators are a potent source and should always be interviewed. And it is always wise, too, to talk to them sooner than later, since it avoids the embarrassment of being told exactly what the trouble is ... after you've spent a lot of time wrestling with test equipment and schematics.

Another powerful reason to use operators as an information source is that they create many of the troubles themselves; that is, many troubles are operator induced. Operators leave switches and valves in the wrong position, spill gunk into the works, or simply use incorrect procedures. Troubleshooters who don't have enough savvy to talk to the operators can waste huge amounts of time tracing their way to troubles that could have been located almost instantly.

3. Troubleshooting Aids

Equipment is usually accompanied by some sort of operator's manual and occasionally also by something in the way of a troubleshooting guide. Where these exist, they can be useful sources of information.

One common type of troubleshooting aid is the *If/Then* page listing symptoms in a left-hand column and probable causes in a right-hand column. The troubleshooter needs only to check the symptoms against the list to determine whether it is possible to go directly to the trouble. Another form of aid is the troubleshooting *tree*, a flowchart type of diagram that walks the troubleshooter through a series of If/Then situations to the trouble.

Such troubleshooting aids provide the trouble sleuth with direct connections between symptoms and trouble. They are also a way to store information in a more permanent and less distortable medium than the troubleshooter's head. Another prime advantage of these aids is that, when properly designed, they require minimum skills to interpret.

4. The Equipment

If the troubleshooter doesn't already know where a trouble is located, and if the operator or a troubleshooting aid can't or won't tell, then it is necessary to ask the equipment itself for information. Many kinds of modern equipment are designed to troubleshoot themselves to a large degree. They provide telltales (lights, flags, meters) that either tell exactly what the trouble is or that can be easily interpreted by the troubleshooter. When our office copier ceases to function, for example, a light often comes on that says, "Add toner" or "Add paper"; it tells us exactly what the trouble is and what to do about it. Computer troubleshooters can often "run a diagnostic," a program that exercises the system, identifies discrepancies between what IS and what OUGHT TO BE, and displays this information on a screen.

5. The Search

What happens if the troubleshooter's experience doesn't point the way to a trouble? Or the operator or the troubleshooting aids or the equipment itself? When the trouble location isn't available from these direct sources of information, the troubleshooter is forced *as a last resort* to use systematic search procedures. Ironically, it is these last resort procedures that are usually referred to as troubleshooting, while the most direct and efficient means of locating troubles are seldom thought of as part of the troubleshooting process.

Because systematic hunting procedures are harder to learn, instructors spend most of their time teaching them. The novice troubleshooter then gets the distinct impression that these are the procedures to follow when searching for troubles. Students seldom, if ever, are told that these systematic analytical procedures are to be used only if more direct sources of information have been tapped and found wanting.

A variety of documents are available to assist in this search, some simple and some highly sophisticated. The most sophisticated provide a carefully designed sequence of hunting steps; they are easiest for the troubleshooter to use because they require the least amount of knowledge to interpret. The documents least useful to the troubleshooter are usually those that are most useful to the equipment designer. But more about the search later.

6. The Hotshot

What happens when all of the above fail to lead to the trouble? If good fortune is smiling, the troubleshooter is able to call a hotshot, a highly experienced individual who knows everything about the equipment and has either personally experienced the rare troubles or can recall the experiences of others who have. One of these people is almost always available for consultation, either in person or by telephone.

SUMMARY SO FAR

- The purpose of troubleshooting is to return equipment to operational status as rapidly as possible by whatever means are available.

- Troubleshooting includes trouble locating (information collecting) and trouble clearing (replacement, adjustment, repairing).
- Efficient troubleshooting strategy (the general approach) is similar for all equipment, but the tactics (the specific procedures) change according to the equipment, available test equipment, and troubleshooting aids.
- The essence of troubleshooting is to change the odds of trouble location from equal or high probability to certainty.
- Information sources available to the troubleshooter usually include personal experience, the equipment operator, troubleshooting aids, the equipment itself, the search procedure, and a highly experienced hotshot.
- An efficient troubleshooting strategy directs the troubleshooter to access information sources from most to least productive.

AND NOW?

To detect discrepancies between what IS and what OUGHT TO BE in the teaching of troubleshooting, you need to be able to tell the difference between *efficient* and *inefficient* troubleshooting strategies. Then you can determine whether or not a strategy being taught is consistent with the state of the art and can spot opportunities for improvement. Toward that end, it is useful to review what some of the research literature has to say on the subject and to listen to the wisdom of some experienced troubleshooters.

Competent
Troubleshooters
(For Better or Worse)

> *"How did you know the trouble was in the switch?"*
> *he asked.*
> *"Because it worked intermittently when I jiggled the*
> *switch."*
> *"Well—couldn't it jiggle the wire?"*
> *"No ..."*
> *"How do you know all that?"*
> *"It's obvious."*
> *"Well then, why didn't I see it?"*
> *"You have to have some familiarity."*
> *"Then it's not obvious, is it?"* [1]

As "everyone knows," things are obvious ... if you happen to be able to see them. And so it is with common sense. A

---

[1] Robert M. Pirsig, *Zen and the Art of Motorcycle Maintenance* (New York: William Morrow and Company, Inc., 1974), p. 124.

marvelous commodity. But sense is only common to those who have it, and those who have it tend to forget how they got it.

IT'S COMMON SENSE

It's common sense to look both ways before crossing the street. Oh, why? Well, to get to the other side safely. It's common sense to take off your mittens before playing the piccolo. Why? Because you can't put your fingers over the holes if you don't. It's common sense to check whether the TV is plugged in before troubleshooting the circuitry. Why? Because you will probably waste a lot of time—and look pretty dumb—if you don't.

"Wait a minute," you may be thinking, "I thought he was going to tell me about the differences between good and poor troubleshooters. Now here he is going on about common sense."

Good point. I was wondering about that myself. But when I sat down to summarize my notes on those differences, I was struck by the number of times the experienced troubleshooters used that expression and also by the fact that what these troubleshooters do as a matter of common sense is so seldom done by the less competent troubleshooters.

What are those common sense behaviors that differentiate the experienced from the inexperienced? Here are the three main ones.

- Experienced troubleshooters talk with operators and listen to them carefully; the inexperienced don't.
- Experienced troubleshooters check for common troubles (unplugged plugs, poor adjustments and alignments); the inexperienced don't.
- Experienced troubleshooters attempt quick fixes (reset controls, interlocks) regardless of the symptoms; the inexperienced don't.

There are four other differences that may not be so easy to categorize as common sense.

- Experienced troubleshooters don't head for their reference materials early or frequently, and they don't spend long periods of time reading them; the inexperienced do.
- Experienced troubleshooters don't spend much time looking for checkpoints and components; the inexperienced do.
- Once they have identified what they are sure is the trouble, experienced troubleshooters aren't reluctant to try a solution right away; the inexperienced are.
- Experienced troubleshooters don't tend to repeat the same tests; the inexperienced do.

Those are the major differences between what the experienced and the inexperienced troubleshooters *do*, the differences in their troubleshooting behavior. There are also some differences in the results of their efforts. The experienced troubleshooters are

- more *proficient* (locate more troubles)
- more *efficient* (locate troubles using fewer checks and spares).

IT'S UNCOMMON SENSE

Well, you might think, those differences should be expected. After all, doesn't experience help us get better at doing things? Isn't experience the *best* teacher? Isn't it reasonable to expect that on-the-job experience will improve almost anyone's performance? Isn't that what the on-the-job learning curve is all about? Mmmm. Well, yes and no. It just isn't as simple as that.

Let me try it this way. Suppose you enroll in my course in basket weaving, and you spend the first three weeks studying the theory of weaving. Then, during the next couple of weeks, I have you practice reading basket weaving diagrams, and that's followed by a week of practice in spotting errors on those diagrams. After which I hand you your diploma and you head out for your first job ... where you do some terrible basket weaving. Six months later, though, you are terrific, as you have had a lot of practice on the job (instead of at my school where it belonged). We could draw one helluva learning curve to show your progress from no proficiency to high proficiency. But wouldn't that learning curve be an artifact of my poorly designed instruction? Wouldn't it show that you were forced to learn on the job what you should have been taught at school?

Would you still say that an on-the-job learning curve is a necessary fact of life because experience is the *best* teacher? Although experienced troubleshooters are more competent than the inexperienced, can their experience only be acquired on the job? Certainly not. A well-designed course can provide faster and more reliable experience than can time on the job. That's what a course is for.

RESEARCH ON COMPETENCE VS. INCOMPETENCE

There is a small mountain of research on troubleshooting, but most of it has to do with studying the usefulness of specific strategies and test equipment in special situations, such as the troubleshooting of circuit boards and power lines. What follows is about all that research has to say about differences between competent and less competent troubleshooters.

Radar

In 1958, Robert Baldwin of the Human Resources Research Organization reported the results of performance tests given to newly graduated AAFCS M-33 Radar mechanics and to their field-experienced counterparts.[2] (This radar was the father of

---

[2] Robert D. Baldwin et al., *The AAFCS M-33 Mechanic Proficiency Test: Part I—Comparison of Mechanics With and Without Field Experience; Part II—Development and Cross-Validation*, Technical Report 38 (Alexandria, Va.: Human Resources Office, May 1958).

the one that was used to control the Nike missile system and was housed mainly in a large van.) The three-hour examination was based on a series of faults that were placed into a functioning radar. The testee was shown one symptom in the way it might typically be reported, and the subsequent troubleshooting behavior was recorded by a trained observer who provided no clues about the possible location of the trouble and who interfered only if the testee was about to do something dangerous. The experienced mechanics were tested in exactly the same way as the new graduates except that they were tested on the equipment they normally maintained in the field. The differences were interesting and substantial.

If you had watched this testing (as I did), you would have been struck by the fact that the experienced people began their troubleshooting by operating the equipment. They checked the position of controls and noted the results of control manipulation because they had learned that a significant percentage of the troubles they were called on to repair were caused by operators who left controls in the wrong position, forgot about them, and then called for help when they thought the system was "broke." In addition, the experienced troubleshooters had learned that other symptoms spotted by control manipulation would help them localize and sometimes even clear the trouble.

On the other hand the new graduates tended to run right to their schematics and spend large amounts of time poring over them . . . as though they expected the answer to pop out at them. Of course that's exactly what they had been taught to do, so no one should have been surprised that they did it.

Another difference: as the experienced mechanics checked controls they also attempted quick fixes. They banged interlocked doors to make sure they were operating properly; they jiggled tubes in their sockets (remember vacuum tubes?); they reseated connectors. And this was because they had learned from experience that some troubles are caused by things jarring loose. The inexperienced mechanics headed for their schematics.

Another difference had to do with parts location. The new graduates spent considerably more time hunting for checkpoints and components. Furthermore, almost half the new graduates were totally unable to locate within *ten* minutes a portion of the equipment that consumed about half a cubic yard of space. This was because their instruction had emphasized schematic reading and circuit tracing and forgotten to teach them the location of the items shown on the diagrams.

Finally, the inexperienced mechanics hesitated before attempting solutions, even though they felt certain they had located the trouble. The experienced had more courage of their convictions and were more prone to try solutions. This might seem a reasonable difference between experience and inexperience, but once again, this habit was caused by faulty instruction. During troubleshooting practice, trainees were required to verbally justify their attempted solutions. They had been embarrassed by nasty comments from the instructor if they couldn't "prove" that the solution they were about to attempt was correct.

An interesting comment was made on a *non*difference. It was reported that the use of test equipment does *not* increase with an increase in proficiency. Some highly proficient troubleshooters used their test equipment a great deal, while others used it hardly at all.

Computers

In 1978, Hemphill and Wescourt published a report on training people to debug (troubleshoot) computer programs.[3] Its four informal conclusions about the least competent debuggers said that they

---

[3]Linda Hemphill and Keith T. Wescourt, *Representing and Teaching Knowledge for Troubleshooting/Debugging*, report prepared for the Office of Naval Research and the Advanced Research Projects Agency (Stanford, Ca.: Institute for Mathematical Studies and Social Sciences, Stanford University, February 1978).

- were not very good at program testing because they did not have a well-practiced procedure for doing so
- did not collect or use all the available information on the effects of a bug
- were hesitant about attempting minor and sometimes seemingly illogical repairs
- did not use unsuccessful repair attempts as a source of information about what to do next.

Here again we see a pattern. More proficient computer program troubleshooters collect more of the available information, and they try more solutions.

Medical Diagnosis

People in medicine refer to medical diagnosis as problem solving rather than troubleshooting (they probably don't want to be thought of as people mechanics), but it's pretty much the same thing. Symptoms of a problem are presented, and the problem solver (diagnostician, troubleshooter) tries to locate the cause. There is one difference, though. Equipment troubleshooters know there is always a solution; if the equipment used to work properly, there must be a way to make it work that way again—unless it is worn out. Medical diagnosticians aren't in such an enviable position. Sometimes they identify problems for which there are no known solutions.

What does research say about the differences between competent and less competent medical diagnosticians? A 1978 study by Elstein et al.[4] tried to identify the differences by observing the behavior of twenty-four physicians who were asked to diagnose eleven problems presented by "patients." The patients were really actors trained to respond to questions according to the diseases or conditions selected for them. The researchers reconstructed the reasoning processes used by the physicians and made note of their more visible behaviors.

---

[4]Authus S. Elstein, Lee S. Shulman, and Sarah A. Srafka, *Medical Problem Solving* (Cambridge, Mass.: Harvard University Press, 1978).

Results? The more successful diagnosticians had more prior knowledge in their memories than the less successful ones. Though both types seemed to be doing the same things when conducting a diagnosis, the more successful ones had more information at their disposal to do it with.

Thus we see once again that good knowledge of past events (in our case, common troubles) is one key to competent performance. Although troubleshooters are often forced to gain that knowledge through experience, their competence could be improved faster if knowledge of common troubles were provided during their instruction.

A 1979 study by Cutler[5] made an observation about the importance of probability information by offering three maxims for diagnosticians:

- Common diseases occur commonly.
- Uncommon manifestations of common diseases are more common than common manifestations of uncommon diseases.
- No disease is rare to the person who has it.

It is interesting to translate these maxims into the language of equipment troubleshooting. They come out this way:

- Common troubles occur frequently.
- Unusual symptoms of common troubles occur more often than common symptoms of uncommon troubles (that is, unusual symptoms are more likely to lead to common troubles than common symptoms are likely to lead to rare troubles).
- No trouble is rare to the client who has it.

Auto Repair

One more study had a little to say about differences between competent and less competent troubleshooters. Though this

---

[5]Paul Cutler, *Problem Solving in Clinical Medicine* (Baltimore: Williams and Wilkins Company, 1979).

1971 research by Finch[6] didn't address itself specifically to the topic of differences, it did indicate that the more successful auto mechanics were

- less redundant (they repeated checks or tests less often than the less successful mechanics)
- more efficient (they made fewer checks or tests to locate the trouble).

TROUBLESHOOTERS ON COMPETENCE VS. INCOMPETENCE

Experienced troubleshooters themselves are another source of information. Many of them have worked with, or tried to train, novice troubleshooters, and they have war stories to tell about "Incompetents I Have Known." Let's listen to a few of them and then summarize the differences they have found between the good troubleshooters and the not-so-good ones.

Appliance Repair

I talked with a man who had just retired after a long career in radio, TV, and appliance repair about his troubles in transferring his skills to employees. This is the gist of that conversation.

"It's always hard to find people with common sense. It was never hard to find people, but it was hard to find people who would use their heads when they were troubleshooting. We experienced hands knew that if you take the time to talk with the woman, she'll tell you where the trouble is. Oh, not in so many words, maybe; but if you have enough sense to listen, she'll lead you to it. But these young guys, they wanted to run right to the machine and take it apart. Heck, that's the *last* thing they should do.

---

[6]Curtis R. Finch, *Troubleshooting Instruction in Vocational-Technical Education via Dynamic Simulation*, final report, PDE Projects 10064, 19-1024 (Harrisburg: Pennsylvania Department of Education, August 1971).

"They just wouldn't do the obvious, like cleaning the spider webs, bugs, and dust out of a television set before getting out their test equipment. Sometimes I used to think they believed that those test probes were magic wands that would point to troubles, and I had a heck of a time teaching them to keep their hands off the test equipment until they had checked the obvious — the dirt, the controls, the antennas. Heck, you could clear more than eighty percent of the troubles in a radio or television set just by cleaning it and maybe changing a tube. But no, that was too demeaning to the young guys. They wanted to *troubleshoot*."

Apartment Maintenance

After retiring from an army career during which he managed radar maintenance schools, this man now supervises the appliance maintenance of more than 250 apartment complexes. He's one of those hotshots who can fix almost anything.

"It's easy to spot the ten-cent bumblers. Instead of talking with the client, they take out the motor. Some of them don't even bother to make sure they have the right apartment before heading for the appliance. We've had some pretty surprised tenants when a mechanic showed up to fix an appliance they didn't even own.

"They head right for the appliance without even verifying the symptoms. 'Take out the motor,' that's their motto. I'm not sure why they do that. Maybe they're looking for a place to use the three-finger rule they learned in school.

"We've had some maintenance men working for fifteen years who have never been up on a roof to check the air conditioners. Preventive maintenance is one of the things the ten-cent bumblers don't do. They just automatically replace the air conditioner every six years, whether it needs it or not. These guys aren't paid much, but they sure are expensive."

"Isn't there a school for appliance maintenance?" I asked.

"Sure there is," he replied. "But they don't teach a practical troubleshooting procedure. They teach 'em how to rewind motors but not how to clear the common troubles. For example, one of the most common things that happens to a dishwasher is that a utensil will chip the enamel. If you don't do anything about it, the thing will rust clean through. It isn't hard to epoxy the rust spots ... just a simple fix that will lengthen the life of the machine. But they don't teach that in the school. They teach 'em how to rewind motors."

"OK," I said, "what do the competent ones do?"

"That's easy to answer. They do their preventive maintenance. They check and verify symptoms rather than barge in and start taking things apart. They talk to the tenants, trying to get them to verbalize the start-up procedure they follow so they can tell whether they're dealing with an operator-caused problem or something else. They look for the obvious; that is, they'll stand there and look at the machine for a bit. They'll check the controls, jiggle a wire here and there, and then try to operate it. They save their signal tracing as a last resort."

Big Equipment

Then there is the hotshot hydraulic press troubleshooter who flies from the home office to customers when their equipment goes down.

"They insist that I come in person because down time is costing them $35,000 an hour. But that's not a good reason.

Why, if they let me talk to the operator by phone, I can clear some troubles in a few minutes. And if they let me talk to their on-site maintenance people I can clear most of them by phone. Know why it's so easy? Because most of their troubles are caused by a lack of ordinary care. The client's staff of maintenance people just don't do their preventive maintenance, and a little fifty-cent filter will get clogged. The mill goes down, they send the operator home, and then they scream for me to fly out on the first available.

"It's sometimes hard to get people to understand that preventive maintenance routines are there because they're important. And you know, it's the same plants that go down over and over again. It isn't the equipment. It's the maintenance people who don't do their PMs. You can spot 'em every time."

Shortly after interviewing this troubleshooter, I talked with another one who handles big equipment, a chief troubleshooter for a manufacturer of paper mills.

"Just last week I saw a good example of the difference between competent and incompetent troubleshooting. The mill went down and the local crew tried their darndest to get it running. They knew the trouble was in a motor, but they couldn't find exactly what was wrong with it. After two days they called us and I sent a man down. He looked around the plant and saw an old motor sitting in a corner. He dusted it off, jerry-rigged it into the mill, and off it went. The local guys had forgotten that their function wasn't fixing the motor, but getting the mill UP and running.

"I think that's one of the differences between the good ones and the poor ones. The good ones remember why they're there. The poor ones spend a lot of time trying to clear a specific trouble instead of trying to get the machine back in service. If they were smart, they'd get the machine running as fast as possible and then try to clear the trouble from whatever they replaced . . . or send it up to the next level for them to clear."

Oil Wells

"You end up tasting a lot of things when you're troubleshooting an oil well or a producing well," said an experienced man from some oil fields in Canada. "You even taste in a steam generating plant."

"Taste what?" I asked.

"Water," he said. "If the water tastes funny, you know you've got problems."

"Funny how?" I asked. I was full of clever questions.

"If it tastes like anything but distilled water, it's a symptom of trouble somewhere in the system."

"What about wells?"

"If they kill the well [overpressure it], when the water goes from fresh to salt you know you are getting your kill fluid [reservoir water] back."

"Tell me about the difference between good and not-so-good troubleshooters," I prompted.

"Well, the good ones are more likely to try things. The new ones are more timid. They spend more time testing and collecting information, but they don't collect information by changing things. For example, on process equipment like a refinery, the good troubleshooters will bounce the process around. They'll change the pressure, change the flow, that sort of thing. They'll push the flow beyond the design limits to bring the problem to light."

"Something like smoke-testing electrical and electronic equipment?"

"Exactly."

"How are these good troubleshooters trained?"

"They aren't trained. They just grow. In the oil world they think a good troubleshooter is born, not trained. He has X-ray vision and super taste buds. But, in fact, people grow into the troubleshooting role by being around the site for so long they know all the common troubles and what to do about them."

"Could any of that be taught?" I asked.

"Of course it could."

Personal Computers

"The new ones even get the customers' equipment mixed up," said a very competent troubleshooter of personal computers. "Worse," she added, "they'll take two or three machines apart at once and then not follow through."

"Are there other differences?" I asked.

"Yes," she replied. "They jump to conclusions. They don't check or verify their symptoms. Instead, they start 'fixing.' They just don't have a plan — they don't follow a troubleshooting method.

"They don't eyeball either. They don't look around for the obvious — things like loose wires or unseated chips. You know, most of the troubles are mechanical — things like disk drive adjustments or dirty heads. But the new guys don't look for those."

"Do you get many machines with operator-induced troubles?"

"About a third of the so-called troubles are operator problems. We get to 'fix' the video monitor that's perfect except that the video gain has been turned down, and they bring us printers that would work fine if the baud rate switch were in the right position. But the new troubleshooters seem to have to learn the simple things the hard way."

"How did you learn to troubleshoot?" I asked.

"Experience. I learned theory in school, but I didn't learn anything about troubleshooting method or get any troubleshooting practice there. I learned all that on the job."

SUMMARY

You can see a lot of similarity in what research and experienced troubleshooters say about the differences between competent and less competent troubleshooters. Competent troubleshooters

- talk to the operators
- verify symptoms

- attempt quick fixes on the basis of their knowledge of common troubles
- repeat checks and tests less often
- know where checkpoints and components are located
- attempt solutions when they have a good idea
- save signal tracing as the last source of information.

In short, the order in which they access sources of information about trouble location approximates the most to least productive.

On the other hand, less effective troubleshooters tend to do the opposite. They run to their schematic diagrams *first* rather than last, and they often fail to access useful information from such productive sources as operators, symptom verifications, and quick fixes.

NEXT?

Now it is time to draw an ideal troubleshooting strategy on paper by charting the strategy of the masters. With this picture of an ideal strategy in hand, you will be able to spot and make those changes needed to fit it to your equipment and your environment.

You will develop an efficient troubleshooting strategy (general approach) that is similar to the ideal, but your tactics (specific steps) will vary to match your equipment and circumstances. You will then be able to compare the strategy that IS being taught in your courses with what OUGHT TO BE taught and spot opportunities for improvement.

3

An Ideal Troubleshooting Strategy

(The Master's Touch)

With your troubleshooting experience you are an old hand at reading a variety of block and schematic diagrams, as well as troubleshooting trees. So, what we are going to do now will be right up your alley, as it is time to draw a model flowchart depicting an ideal troubleshooting strategy.* Then you will be able to make changes in this model that will turn it into a flowchart showing the ideal procedure for troubleshooting your equipment in your situation, giving you your first course-troubleshooting tool.

The model strategy to be depicted represents a composite drawn from research findings and from procedures used by highly competent and experienced troubleshooters of a wide

---

*If you just can't wait to see it, you'll find it on page 50.

variety of equipment. First I'll describe it step by step, and then I'll show you the flowchart depicting those steps.

WHAT COMPETENT TROUBLESHOOTERS DO

Because of the variety of items they are expected to maintain, troubleshooters do and use different things. Some use screwdrivers, while others use oscilloscopes, stethoscopes, voltmeters, or wiring diagrams. Some spend a great deal of time disassembling in order to gain access to test points or adjustments, and others spend none. Some require access to large amounts of documentation, while others need only a page.

But whatever the nature of the equipment to be fixed, and the equipment used to accomplish that purpose, competent troubleshooters don't differ so much by WHAT they do, but rather by HOW they go about doing it. The strategy (the approach) is pretty much the same for all equipment; only the tactics (the steps for implementing the strategy) differ.

Here's what competent troubleshooters do, in the approximate order in which they do it.

1. Talk With the Operator

Operators are the richest potential source of information about what is wrong and where the trouble is, and competent troubleshooters always talk to the operators when they are available. Operators were there when it happened, they generally know what they and the equipment were doing when it happened, and they know what happened that was different from normal operation.

"There was a little puff of smoke right over there."
"I pressed this button and it went 'clankety-clank.'"
"I tried to run the program but it only printed gibberish."
"It won't start no matter what I do."
"The picture is all crinkly."

This information tells competent troubleshooters a great deal about what is wrong and where.

Sometimes the operator isn't that helpful.

"The damn thing's busted again."

"I said something to it and now it won't work right."

"I think I hurt its feelings."

Very often, however, the operator can tell the troubleshooter exactly what and where the trouble is. When that happens, other troubleshooting steps can be avoided; the troubleshooter merely verifies the symptoms and clears the trouble.

"This rod is bent."

"This cam has worn down again."

"This belt broke."

"The connector is loose on this cable."

While sometimes wrong or not too helpful, operators are still the most potent source of information available, and competent troubleshooters head for the operator as a first step.

2. Verify Symptoms

Immediately after their interview with the operator, competent troubleshooters verify symptoms. They know that hearing of or seeing a symptom is not automatic proof of a malfunction. Just because equipment doesn't work properly doesn't mean something is wrong with it. Suppose an operator forgot to turn it on or plug it in? Suppose a switch or a valve were left in the wrong position? Operators are notorious for being a source of troubles, and competent troubleshooters know it is inefficient and potentially embarrassing to break out test equipment and sophisticated analytical procedures before verifying the symptoms.

Before television there was only radio. When a radio malfunctioned it was taken by its owner to the radio repair shop, plopped on the counter, and its symptoms were described. Often a customer would complain about a "hissing radio."

"It doesn't work any more," the owner would complain. "It just hisses and makes crackling sounds, but it doesn't get any stations."

Now the minute the customer said "hisses" the troubleshooter would casually turn the radio around, look at the back, and verify the "trouble." Sure enough, there was nothing wrong with the radio. The AM-shortwave switch had been accidentally snapped to the shortwave position by the operator, making reception of AM stations impossible.

Interestingly, from the troubleshooter's point of view, the problem was "How do I switch the switch without making the customer feel foolish?" Generally, the solution was to take the radio to the back room and make the "fix" there or to ask the customer to return the following day.

This is but one classic example of an operator-induced problem. There are many, many others, and experienced troubleshooters can regale you with stories about the times they hunted for troubles that weren't there.

So, competent troubleshooters verify symptoms right away. They determine whether the trouble is real to make sure they don't spend time troubleshooting when they should be instructing an operator about how to avoid the trouble in the future. When the trouble *is* real, symptom verification will often provide additional clues about its location.

But there is more. By operating the equipment, the troubleshooter will often collect more clues about trouble location than were provided by the initially reported symptom. When something goes wrong, it can show up in more ways than one, and troubleshooters who can tell the difference between normal and abnormal operation will spot those clues.

"I do a lot of troubleshooting by telephone," a highly competent troubleshooter of video equipment told me. "When a customer tells me what's wrong I'll have them operate the system for me, if I know it's safe to do so, and tell me what happens. Lots of times I'm able to tell them what's wrong right on the phone. I don't even have to see the equipment." (Let alone rig test equipment.)

No question about it. Competent troubleshooters verify symptoms before digging into the equipment itself.

3. Attempt Quick Fixes

Even before they have located a trouble, competent troubleshooters attempt quick fixes; that is, they attempt solutions that are fast to try, even though they may be illogical in terms of the symptoms presented. They check fuses, adjust controls, push circuit boards firmly into their sockets, clean contacts, clean filters, replace gaskets, vacuum, dust, and bang or kick interlocked doors or cabinets to make sure they are properly seated. They tighten this or reseat that, adjust here or align there. Troubleshooters know that these actions will clear the trouble some of the time, and since they are rapidly accomplished, they are worth doing. If quick fixes work, time and effort have been saved. If they don't work, only a moment has been lost while the information has been gained that certain parts of the equipment, at least, are *not* the cause of the trouble.

Often, troubleshooters engage in these rapid clearing actions while verifying symptoms and looking for other visible signs of malfunction. Auto mechanics, for example, are likely to twist or jiggle spark plug cables while looking about the engine compartment, regardless of the nature of the trouble. They know it is worth doing this since rough engines are sometimes caused by loose, oily, or wet contacts. They scan not only with their eyes but with their hands and ears, and often are totally unaware of what they are doing. Were you to ask, "Why did you do that?" they might very well reply, "Do what?"

In a way, quick fixes are a form of preventive maintenance. In common usage, preventive maintenance means periodic general servicing of equipment, *whether it needs it or not*. As you know, these actions are carried out because they will either lengthen the life of the equipment or increase the amount of time the equipment is operational—they will minimize down time. Competent troubleshooters know that many troubles are caused by skimpy preventive maintenance or a total absence of such routine care. Thus, some of their quick fix actions can be thought of as belated preventive maintenance.

There is another reason for attempting the quick fix or, if you prefer, a reason for attempting solutions without first doing detailed troubleshooting: *Equipment troubles do not occur with equal probability; some are much more likely to occur than others.* Competent troubleshooters know this. They also know which troubles are likely to occur most often and the symptoms associated with those troubles. Moreover, *everybody* knows that some troubles are more common than others. When the table lamp doesn't light we don't begin troubleshooting, we change the bulb. When the car doesn't turn over, we check the battery. It isn't always the battery, and it isn't always the light bulb, but the probability is high that these are the sources of trouble. When they are, it would be inefficient to pretend that these probabilities don't exist, especially when clearing actions are quick and easy to take. It could be costly to pretend that trouble probabilities don't exist and demand that troubleshooters always follow the same procedure for the sake of uniformity or because "the prescribed procedure will eventually lead to the trouble."

Efficient troubleshooting, then, requires that troubleshooters be armed with all available trouble-probability information. Unarmed, they are deprived of a potent tool for rapid trouble isolations. But regardless of what their information is called, competent troubleshooters attempt solutions that are rapid and efficient, because they pay off handsomely either in a trouble cleared or in information gained.

4. Review Troubleshooting Aids

When troubleshooters have talked with the operator, verified symptoms, and tried quick fixes, but still haven't located the fault, additional information must be collected. The troubleshooting aid is the next most efficient source of information to check out. Why? Because such aids offer some prepackaged information that troubleshooters would have to seek elsewhere if the aid were absent.

Of the several types of troubleshooting aids, some are brief and not too helpful, while others are highly sophisticated or even automated. For example, you have the easy-to-interpret "idiot lights" in your automobile that tell you when the oil is too low or when the alternator ceases to provide a suitable charge for the battery. The cockpit of a modern aircraft is loaded with bells, buzzers, and whoopers to indicate various malfunctions and even impending malfunctions. In one fighter aircraft, for example, there is a repeating sound that changes frequency and tempo as gravity forces are built up during a turn. The higher the G forces, the higher and more rapid the sound, telling the pilot of an approaching malfunction — in this case, DOOM. The sound monitors a stress condition of the aircraft, and from listening the pilot knows whether or not a correction is needed. In this case, there is no need to talk with an operator, to collect additional symptoms, or to try quick fixes — other than the one suggested by this troubleshooting aid.

More and more modern equipment is being designed to provide direct information about troubles. Sensors detect troubles that are then reported by lights, sounds, and other forms of information display. These aids are a response to the growing complexity of some types of equipment, but reflect what is still a growing technology. Though immensely useful, it is still possible for the telltales themselves to fail, making the troubleshooting task even harder than before. Therefore, the importance of providing troubleshooters with other well-designed aids is still as strong as ever.

A sometimes overlooked troubleshooting aid is the "Caution" information attached to the equipment itself. "Caution: Remove all red tags before operating" is one example. "Caution: High voltage in this compartment" is another. True, true, these aids don't help in *locating* troubles, but they do help to save the equipment and the troubleshooters from early demise.

Still another type of aid is the If/Then page, typically describing symptoms on the left and suggested actions on the right. You may find aids like this in the owner's manual that came with your automobile and the instructions accompanying your appliances. They tell you what the common troubles are and what to do about them. Similar troubleshooting aids may be provided with more sophisticated equipment, and some maintenance people construct their own.

Related to these are the troubleshooting trees, a type of flowchart that walks the troubleshooter through a series of actions and decision points, hopefully to the trouble. Often called "fully proceduralized troubleshooting aids," these aids are a thinking prompt, a form of prepackaged analysis intended to relieve the troubleshooter of the need to memorize all the steps to follow. Well-constructed aids of this type do indeed improve the speed and accuracy with which faults are located, even by the inexperienced troubleshooter. At least one study[1] among several comparing the usefulness of proceduralized troubleshooting aids with more traditionally constructed maintenance manuals showed these aids to be better than the manuals. More troubles were located, and inexperienced troubleshooters made as few errors as experienced people. This should be expected, as the fully proceduralized troubleshooting aid is a carefully constructed and tested way of guiding the troubleshooter to the source of the problem. Troubleshooters have to know more about the system in order to make good use of traditional maintenance manuals. In addition to knowing the geography of the system, they need more specific troubleshooting knowledge to make up for the

---

[1]John P. Foley, Jr., *Impact of Advance Maintenance Data and Task Oriented Training Technologies on Maintenance, Personnel and Training Systems,* AFHRL-TR-78-25 (Brooks Air Force Base, Texas: Air Force Human Resources Laboratory, September 1978).

incomplete or inaccurate information in the manual. *In short, it takes higher aptitude (smarter) people to use the typical maintenance manuals because those manuals are designed as information sources about how things work rather than as troubleshooting aids.*

Then there are the sophisticated diagnostics — aids used in locating malfunctions in computers and similar equipment. They don't require the troubleshooter's assistance at all, except to initiate the diagnostic operation. Diagnostics are programs designed to exercise a system, to note discrepancies between normal and abnormal operation, and to report the nature and often the exact source of the trouble either on a video display or printer (for example, "Bad RAM at C5").

When troubleshooting aids exist, experienced troubleshooters use the ones that remind them about efficient paths to follow for information collection, or those that report specific troubles. They don't use aids containing information they have already memorized through practice and experience, and they don't use aids that are poorly designed.

5. Step-by-Step Search

When other sources of information fail to reveal the trouble source, troubleshooters turn to a step-by-step search through the equipment itself. This is the last resort of competent troubleshooters, however, as it is the least time-efficient system of information gathering when compared to other information sources. This isn't to say that the step-by-step search is therefore unimportant; it is only to say that this procedure (oddly referred to as "systematic," "analytical," or "logical" troubleshooting) is used by competent people only after all other information sources fail.

Several step-by-step search procedures might be used. A *random search* could be a way to test and replace components, and troubles would eventually be cleared. Unfortunately, since as many troubles would be located later as well as sooner, this approach is used only by the uninformed. A *sequential search* involves systematic testing, starting from one end of the equipment and working item by item to the other end. Although this procudure will also lead eventually to the trouble it, too, is inefficient, because troubles at the far end of the equipment take a long time to get to.

The preferred search procedure is one that yields the most information for the least effort; that is, the most information per action — such as per test check or per trial replacement. Ideally, this search procedure is one that successively eliminates half the system as a possible trouble source. Called the *split-half*, or *half-split search*, the procedure involves successively testing the system at or near its midpoint. When a test shows normal operation, then the portion of the system preceding that point is considered OK and is eliminated from suspicion. By successively eliminating approximately half of the remaining system with each test, the trouble is located more efficiently than with a random or sequential search.

Four points must be made. First, it is seldom possible to test a system exactly at the midpoint of the next section to be checked. No matter. The object is to test at a point each time that will eliminate a large chunk of the system from the suspicion that the trouble may be lurking there.

Second, some systems lend themselves to rapid replacement of large segments containing a large number of components, such as chassis or circuit boards. Such board swapping can quickly isolate the trouble to the replaced unit or eliminate it from suspicion. And even though the swapping might have been done at some distance from a midpoint, the speed with which it is done makes the procedure useful.

Third, the split-half search is used only when a troubleshooter must adopt the equal-probability hypothesis, "As far as I know right now, the trouble could be anywhere." Competent troubleshooters *stop* using this search procedure as soon as (a) they develop an idea worth testing, or (b) when the trouble is located. Once they know or strongly suspect the trouble location, they are likely to test or replace the suspected component or assembly. If they find the trouble, they fix it. If they don't find it, and all other information sources have proven inadequate, they resume the split-half search until they can attempt a fix.

Finally, those skilled in the step-by-step search (called signal tracing for electrical and electronic equipment, flow tracing for hydraulic equipment, and linkage tracing for mechanical equipment) need to have considerable knowledge. They need to be able to read diagrams, use test equipment, interpret waveforms, and locate components and test points. This explains why often it is considerably more economical to have two types of troubleshooters: those who can isolate a trouble to a unit, such as a gearbox, transmission, circuit board, or card; and those who can trace the trouble to the defective component within the unit. The former can generally clear more than eighty percent of the troubles they encounter after very little training, making it very expensive to insist that every troubleshooter be as knowledgeable as those who can clear most or all of the troubles ever encountered.

6. Clear Trouble

Once a trouble is located, someone is expected to eliminate it. Often trouble clearing is done by the troubleshooter, but sometimes it is assigned to someone else. The master auto mechanic, for example, does the diagnosis, but then may assign the actual repair work (trouble clearing) to someone else. The chief engineer at a radio or TV station may be called in to troubleshoot, and then turn the trouble-clearing activity over to the on-duty engineer. Manufacturers' hotshot troubleshooters who travel to clients' locations to solve difficult problems often leave the actual trouble clearing to the local staff.

Trouble clearing is different from trouble locating, and locating requires a different set of skills than clearing. These facts have implications for the content of the troubleshooting course.

7. Perform Preventive Maintenance

As you know, preventive maintenance is the process of clearing troubles before they happen, a process that good troubleshooters perform as regularly and carefully as time and policy permit. They know that doing a PM is more than just a ritual or just another company policy; they know that preventive maintenance saves a great deal of time and money and reduces equipment down time (something the equipment users are very fond of).

It is appropriate to do a PM on some machines even before starting to hunt for the trouble. A PM is usually fast and may clear the trouble. But for most machines, a PM is carried out after the trouble has been cleared. One troubleshooter I talked with explained it this way: "Look, when the customer's machine is down and the plant has come to a grinding halt, they don't want to see my troubleshooters oiling and greasing. They want that equipment UP and running! The oiling and greasing are done after the equipment is operational."

8. Make Final Checks

Competent troubleshooters always check to make sure the trouble is actually cleared and the system is functioning normally. They know too well how easy it is to insert a new trouble while clearing an old one. They know how easy it is to leave something like a setscrew loose, or something unplugged or out of adjustment. Therefore a final check of normal operation is a necessary part of the troubleshooting sequence.

9. Complete Paperwork

Troubleshooters are not immune to the bureaucratic plea to "fill out those forms!" Even though form filling isn't troubleshooting, it is part of the troubleshooter's job. And, this important fact has implications about what the troubleshooting course must teach if it is to produce troubleshooters of maximum service to their organization.

Often the history of a machine is recorded in an equipment log. Dates of PMs, information about retrofits, and parts that have been changed are recorded at the time of service or repair.

Referring to and keeping up a log are two paperwork activities that are part of the maintenance job. Sometimes troubles can be quickly located by simply reading the history in the log, often because the same trouble occurs regularly in that equipment. For this reason the equipment log is a useful source of information, and good troubleshooters take the time to update those logs as well as to refer to them.

10. Inform/Instruct Clients

Once the equipment is returned to service, the client or user is informed of this fact. Often, operators are instructed in the proper use or care of the equipment or cautioned about peculiarities of the system. Although this activity is not strictly part of the troubleshooting procedure, it is important to the continued functioning of the equipment. Further, talking to clients has a definite impact on the image and success of a troubleshooter's employer. Troubleshooters who are rude and insulting or otherwise turn off customers are hardly doing their employers any good. As you can see, these are further implications for the content of the troubleshooting course.

MINI-SUMMARY

The primary purpose of troubleshooting is to return equipment to operational status as quickly as possible, rather than to slavishly follow a given procedure. To accomplish this purpose competent troubleshooters use their knowledge about the system and about the common troubles that occur to that system. To make the best use of their time, they tend to collect information from the best sources available. They:

1. Talk with the operator
2. Verify symptoms

On-Site Troubleshooting

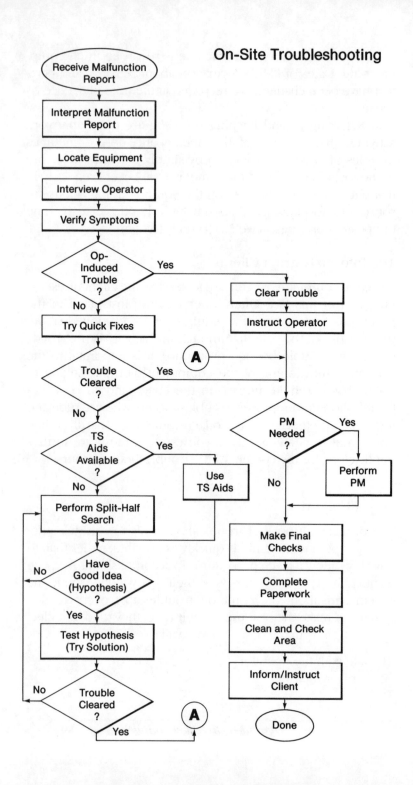

3. Attempt quick fixes
4. Review troubleshooting aids
5. Conduct split-half (step-by-step) search
6. Clear troubles
7. Perform preventive maintenance
8. Make final checks
9. Complete equipment logs and paperwork
10. Inform/instruct clients.

THE TROUBLESHOOTING MODEL

The next step is to review a flowchart* depiction of the action and decision steps in the strategy just described — two flowcharts are provided. The first flowchart represents the troubleshooting procedures followed by someone on site, and the second one shows the steps followed when the troubleshooter begins by telephone. Each chart assumes that the troubleshooter carries out all the activities rather than turn the trouble clearing over to someone else.

On-Site Troubleshooting

Troubleshooters usually receive a report of trouble in the form of a symptom:

"It's jammed again."

"It won't start."

"The dyes are running in the fabric."

After locating the correct machine (and good troubleshooters always make sure they have the right machine), they try to interview the operator.

Unless the machine is jammed or otherwise inoperable, they operate the machine and verify the symptoms collected from the operator.

---

*When a sequence of human actions is flowcharted, it is referred to as a *task analysis*. Although there are a number of task analysis procedures, the flowchart is most effective for depicting the chain of actions and decisions involved in performing a task.

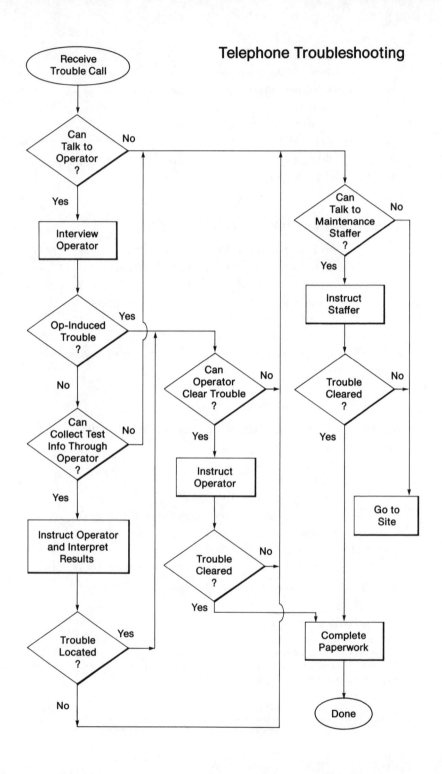

Telephone Troubleshooting

If the problem is operator-induced, they clear it and then instruct the operator in ways to prevent the problem from occurring again.

If the problem is real, they try quick fixes (check interlocks, plugs, and cables; replace units). If any of these works, preventive maintenance may be called for and carried out. Then final checks are made, documentation (paperwork) is completed, the area is cleaned and checked, and the client is informed.

If quick fixes don't solve the problem, troubleshooters follow troubleshooting aids if they are available. If aids are not available, a split-half search procedure is used as a last resort.

When troubleshooters develop a good idea about where or what the trouble is, they test their hypothesis by attempting a solution.

If a solution doesn't work, the search is continued. If it does, troubleshooters complete any preventive maintenance that is indicated and then follow the end steps already described (final check, documentation, area check, and client communication).

Telephone Troubleshooting

Troubleshooters often do a great deal of their troubleshooting over the telephone with the client. This is an effective procedure, because many equipment troubles are operator induced and can be operator cleared. Many other troubles can be cleared by the on-site maintenance staff or by operators. Using the telephone has saved troubleshooters a great deal of unnecessary travel, clients a great deal of money, and trouble inducers a great deal of embarrassment.

Typically, telephone troubleshooters first determine whether the operator is available for consultation. If so, they ask the operator for answers to questions that would indicate that the problem is operator induced:

"Is the red switch in the down position?"
"Is flowmeter A12 showing zero flow?"
"Is it plugged in?"

If the problem is operator induced, the operator is then instructed in the clearing procedure and suggestions are given for avoiding the problem in the future.

If the problem is not operator induced, telephone troubleshooters then try to have someone on-site—operator or maintenance staff—carry out the actions the troubleshooters would carry out if they were there in person. They might ask the person on-site to follow sequences like these: note and report on conditions of key portions of the equipment; report on readings of dials, gauges or meters; or carry out operating steps and report the results.

If procedures like these locate the trouble, then the local maintenance staff is given the task of trouble clearing. However, if the trouble can't be found, a troubleshooter will have to travel to the site, and follow the on-site procedure.

VARIATIONS ON A THEME

Of course, if you observe competent troubleshooters in action, you will not always see them using the most efficient, ideal procedure. Sometimes they use less-than-ideal tactics as a means of dealing with various constraints.

For example, telephone maintenance people are often faced with a trouble referred to as CCIO ("Can't Call In or Out"). Once they have ruled out trouble in the central office as the cause, they are supposed to check the telephone instrument itself to verify that the trouble exists as reported. Then they are supposed to check their way from the instrument toward the telephone exchange until they pinpoint the trouble.

But they don't always do it that way. At one company they always examine the first checkpoint they come to as they are driving toward the customer's telephone, *regardless* of where that point is in the logical chain of test points. Why? Because the cost of operating repair trucks is so high that company policy has been set to follow a more efficient vehicle use procedure. Gas is saved, but the procedure takes longer. Policy says that it is more important to minimize "windshield time" than it is to maximize troubleshooting efficiency.

Or, were you to observe troubleshooters at another plant, you would note that they generally fail to verify their diagnoses with test equipment. Instead, they keep trying different solutions until they succeed in clearing the trouble; they look as though they are changing parts at random. Why? Not because they aren't aware of more efficient troubleshooting procedures, but because the test equipment is awkwardly located some distance away. It is easier for them to test their guesses by changing parts than to take the time and muscle needed to verify a diagnosis. Why is the test equipment kept in the tool crib instead of a location closer to those who need it? It's *always* been done that way.

At a third company, troubleshooters follow a similar procedure, not because the test equipment is relatively inaccessible, but because the schematic diagrams are classified and are kept locked up. It is easier, even though less efficient, to try a string of solutions than to bother signing the schematics out and in.

The variations just described illustrate two types of reasons for deviating from ideal troubleshooting strategy.

1. There is a *sound reason* for deviation. Although the troubleshooting strategy is somewhat less than ideal, it fits a larger plan. There is a good reason for the deviation and it is not inefficient in the context of the larger plan.
2. There is *no sound reason* for deviation. The less-than-ideal strategy is thought to be easier, because "we've *always* done it this way." Little or no thought has been given to how it should be done, and how certain constraints could be better dealt with.

If your troubleshooting strategy deviates from the models shown on the previous pages, the deviations should be for good reasons rather than because "it's always been done this way."

DERIVE YOUR OWN

Now that you have explored two versions of an ideal troubleshooting strategy — on-site and by telephone — it is time to develop a specific troubleshooting procedure that will fit *your equipment* and *your situation*. You will translate ideal strategy into specific tactics appropriate to troubleshooting your equipment and create the first tool for troubleshooting your troubleshooting course.

Here Is What To Do

1. Select the model strategy that best matches the procedure your troubleshooters use in the field.
2. On a piece of paper (flipchart size if possible) write the name of the equipment.
3. Under the name of the equipment, write whether troubleshooters are expected to isolate troubles to a block (chassis, unit, card) or to the faulty component. This will influence the specific troubleshooting steps to be followed.
4. Indicate also whether troubleshooters do or don't have other people such as hotshots to call on for help.
5. Follow the model to build your flowchart. Make your flowchart specific to your equipment and circumstances. Write down the appropriate phone numbers to call, people to talk to, names of the references to use, names of the tools or test equipment to use, and names and/or numbers of required documentation forms.
6. When you have a draft, test it by answering these questions:
   - Did you actually name the equipment? It isn't very helpful to do this in the abstract.
   - Does your flowchart follow the model in each of the key steps?
   - Is your flowchart consistent with the information you wrote at the top of the page?

- Will your troubleshooters actually have the specific items you named in the flowchart?
- If your strategy deviates from the model, can you justify that deviation with a sound reason, such as company policy or other legitimate constraints?

When your flowchart meets the test criteria, you have derived the ideal troubleshooting strategy for your own equipment. You should now be able to troubleshoot the strategy being taught in your course(s).

NEXT?

➠ If you are familiar with the instructional state of the art, at least to some degree, then read on. The next two chapters will show you how to derive the skills that should be taught in a course and how to draw a diagram showing the prerequisite relationships between those skills.

➠ If you are a troubleshooter new to the business of instruction, you may want to read Chapter 7 before you read Chapters 4 and 5. It will draw you a picture of a course operating at the state of the art and will make it easier for you to deal with the next two chapters.

The choice is yours.

PART $\diamondsuit$ 2

Instructional Content

The Skills of Competence
(Sleuthing the Strategy)

Everybody troubleshoots. When your car won't start or your lamp won't light, when your airplane sputters or your refinery leaks, when your antenna goes limp or your cash won't flow, you apply some sort of strategy to locate and eliminate the trouble. But the skills needed to fix a floundering battleship are different from those needed to fix an ailing computer or a stuttering pacemaker. Although the general troubleshooting approach is similar for a wide variety of equipment, the precise skills needed to accomplish the troubleshooting task can differ widely.

For example, though the same troubleshooting strategy may be followed in troubleshooting toasters and TVs, different skills are needed to carry out the specific troubleshooting tactics. TV repair requires some knowledge of electronics; toaster troubleshooting does not. But, along with the different troubleshooting skill requirements, there are also important similarities. No matter what you may be troubleshooting, you need to know how to do it without damaging yourself or the equipment. And, you need to know how to locate components — you can't fix 'em if you can't find 'em!

The purpose of this chapter is to help you derive and list the skills that *anyone* would need before they could apply the troubleshooting procedure depicted by your flowchart. Once you have used the flowchart to derive those skills from the job itself, you will have a second course troubleshooting tool with which to carry out two important review actions.

1. Compare your skill list to course content to determine whether necessary skills are being taught.
2. Compare the skills that troubleshooters must have on the job with those they bring with them to the course; in other words, assess whether the course is teaching what students already know.

DEFINING THE PROCEDURE

This is the procedure for deriving the skills that anyone would need in the performance of the troubleshooting task.

1. Visualize the steps a competent performer follows in an efficient troubleshooting strategy for your equipment. You have already done this in the form of a flowchart.
2. Determine *for each step* of the task the skills that would be needed before someone could *learn that step*. At each step, ask the question, "What skills, if any, must somebody already have to be able to learn how to perform this step?" At a number of steps the answer will be *none*, and at some it will be *more than one*. For example, trainees could start right in learning to "lift wrench," or "use (tool)." On the other hand, before they could learn how to "measure voltage," they would first need to be able to read a meter. And, you would want several prerequisite skills in place before you taught them how to "install control panel" and allowed them to practice that task. Also, the *same* prerequisite skills may be needed before several steps in the strategy can be performed.

3. Write the name of each prerequisite skill beside each strategy step that requires that skill.
4. Delete the duplications.
5. Write your final list.

I am now going to demonstrate this procedure and provide you with a model list of skills to work from.

APPLYING THE PROCEDURE

The procedure will be applied to the troubleshooting strategy shown previously. I'll repeat the on-site flowchart on each page so that you won't have to flip pages. Once you work through this application with me, you will be ready to derive the skills from your own flowchart.

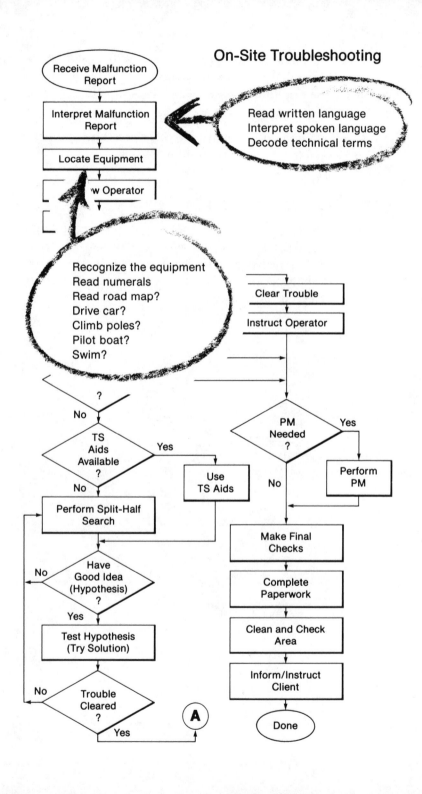

On-Site Troubleshooting

Receive Malfunction Report

Interpret Malfunction Report

Read written language
Interpret spoken language
Decode technical terms

Locate Equipment

w Operator

Recognize the equipment
Read numerals
Read road map?
Drive car?
Climb poles?
Pilot boat?
Swim?

Clear Trouble

Instruct Operator

?

No

TS Aids Available ?

Yes

Use TS Aids

No

Perform Split-Half Search

PM Needed ?

Yes

No

Perform PM

Make Final Checks

Have Good Idea (Hypothesis) ?

No

Yes

Test Hypothesis (Try Solution)

Complete Paperwork

Clean and Check Area

Inform/Instruct Client

No

Trouble Cleared ?

A

Yes

Done

Interpret Malfunction Report

What would *anyone* have to be able to do before learning how to make sense of the malfunction report? Sometimes they need to be able to read a *trouble ticket*, a form on which the trouble is reported. So, they must be able to read English or whatever other language you work in. If trouble reports are received verbally, then troubleshooters need to be able to understand the spoken language. (This is not as trivial as you might think; just think how you react when a waitress or waiter can't understand your language well enough to take your order or when a clerk at the government agency you are calling can't understand or speak English well enough to provide the service you are seeking.)

Therefore, as prerequisite skills for this step, I would list "read written language," "interpret spoken language," and "decode technical terms." Of course, if your troubleshooters aren't required to deal with trouble reports, you won't list any skills for this step.

Locate Equipment

Are any prerequisite skills needed before you would feel ready to teach someone how to locate the equipment needing repair? Troubleshooters need to be able to recognize the equipment when they see it, of course, but you can teach them that directly, can't you? Directly, in that you don't have to require them to be able to do anything else *before* they practice recognizing the equipment to be repaired. Then again, if they are expected to recognize equipment by comparing the number on the hardware to the number on the trouble ticket, they would have to be able to read something. Not everything, but something.

Locating the equipment might also involve traveling to the equipment, and that might imply a need for additional skills. For example, in Arizona some telephone repair people have to be able to ride a horse and climb a pole to get to the equipment needing service. In New York City, however, there

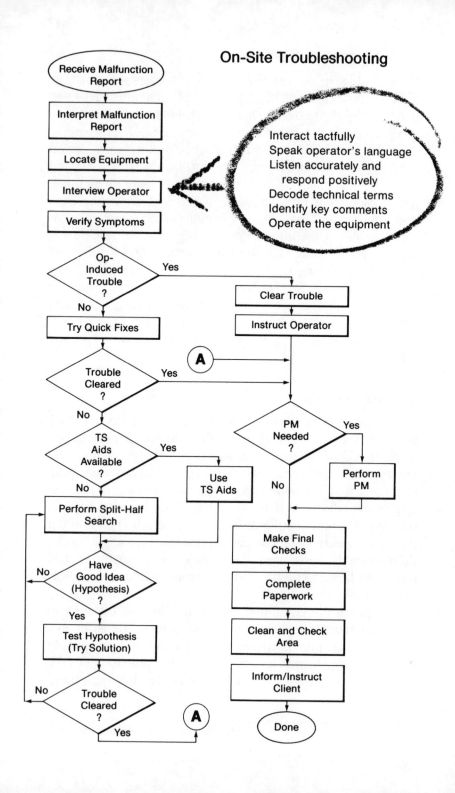

On-Site Troubleshooting

are no poles and so no need for a pole climbing skill. But if your troubleshooters repair marine equipment, they may have to be able to pilot a boat or maybe even swim.

If these points sound trivial to you, it is probably because you are already thinking about what *your* trainees can do when they arrive for instruction, rather than what *anyone* would need to know before performing the troubleshooting task. That is a later step. For the moment try to list what *anyone* needs in the way of skills. Later you will be able to compare your list with what your trainees can already do when they enter training, and the difference will dictate the content of the troubleshooting course for each learner.

Interview Operator

Interacting with others is definitely not a trivial skill, especially if the interaction must be accomplished without angering, insulting, or humiliating the interviewee. What skills are needed before you would allow someone to practice interviewing operators? For one, they would need to speak the language. They can't interview operators who speak only English unless they know that language.

What else? Troubleshooters must also be able to listen to the complaint, respond in a nonthreatening manner, and question without belittling or abrading the other person. If you have ever had to deal with a surly, unconcerned bureaucrat, you know that civil, pleasant, productive interaction is a skill that some people have and some don't.

The consequence of failing to teach this skill was underlined by one of the troubleshooters I interviewed. "Yes," he said, "we've had a number of guys quit because they couldn't take the guff the customers gave them. One guy went out to clear a trouble, and the customer gave him a little static. He didn't know how to handle it, and so he took his toolbox, plunked it down on his manager's desk, and said, 'I quit!'"

(Already you can see the task analysis as a major, powerful source from which to derive course content. By noting that

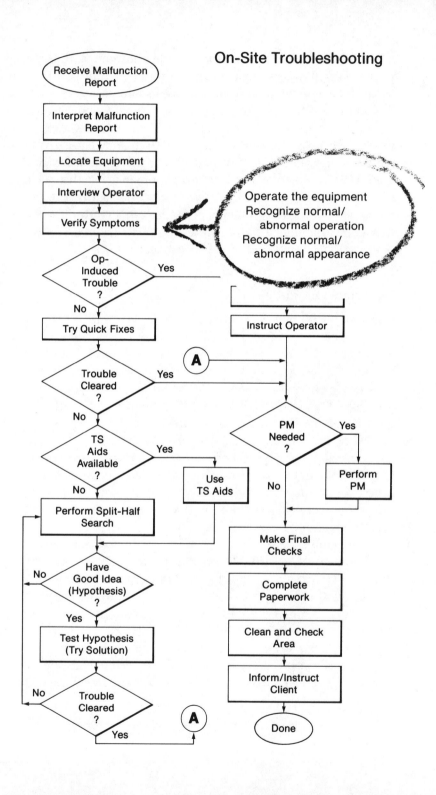

On-Site Troubleshooting

troubleshooters have to be able to communicate with operators you know that interaction skill is essential to the troubleshooting task. You can see that interaction training must be given to those who lack this skill.)

Anything else? Yes, along with the communicating language, the troubleshooter needs to know the special terminology associated with the equipment being described. They can't interact with maximum productivity if they can't interpret the technical terms used. If an operator says, "It always frimples its snerbit when the dorplick blorps," troubleshooters can't make use of that information if they don't know where the snerbit is located or what one looks like when frimpling.*

In addition to technical terms, it is also important to be able to identify the significance of comments and key words offered by the operator, such as:

"It made a funny noise here."

"Sparks came from over there."

"It made an acrid stink."

And to interpret the comments of an operator, troubleshooters also need to be able to operate the equipment. Without an operating skill, they would find it very difficult to make full sense of operator comments.

On the facing page I've listed the skills required for collecting information from informed operators. Armed with these skills, troubleshooters are able to canvass a valuable source of information that might shortcut the troubleshooting process or eliminate it altogether.

Verify Symptoms

The next step in the troubleshooting task is to verify the symptom(s) to make sure the equipment is actually behaving (or misbehaving) as reported. If something has been reported as broken, out of alignment, or leaking, troubleshooters check

---

*Oh, good grief!

that this is the case and then take action accordingly. If the equipment simply isn't working correctly or is putting out a distorted product (such as a mad computer printing gibberish), troubleshooters have to be able to operate the system to verify the symptoms reported, as well as to collect additional information.

Additionally, they need to be able to recognize differences between normal and abnormal operation. Exactly *what* they need to know will, of course, depend on the equipment. Sometimes this is a large learning task and sometimes small. For example, it doesn't take much to learn to recognize a normally operating toaster or microwave oven. It is more difficult to learn to recognize normal/abnormal operation of a computer or missile system.

Depending on the equipment, there may be another skill required here. Suppose an operator hands you a part and says, "This thing fell off. Then the machine began to smoke, so I shut it down." Before operating that machine, you undoubtedly should find out where that part came from and replace it. What would you have to know in order to accomplish that? You would have to know what the equipment looked like when it was in normal condition so you could spot things that weren't right. And to do that you may have to be able to interpret some form of pictorial documentation.

For most equipment, though, symptoms can be verified by troubleshooters who can operate the system and recognize normal/abnormal operation. Do you think it's obvious that troubleshooters need to be able to recognize normal/abnormal operation? I can recall a missile maintenance course that turned out a significant number of graduates who hadn't learned that the system could track a target automatically. Remember when organizing your course, that normal/abnormal operation is not automatically learned as a result of heavy practice in circuit tracing.

When equipment has adjustments that are likely to get out of whack, troubleshooters have to be able to check for

correct adjustments. If adjustments are wrong, then troubleshooters have located a probable source of trouble. Auto
mechanics, for example, will often check the spark plug gap
while verifying symptoms, since gaposis of the spark plug can
add to the severity of other troubles. (Though it may be a
distinction too small to bother about, being able to *check* an
adjustment; that is, to determine whether the adjustment is OK,
is not the same skill as being able to *make* the adjustment.)

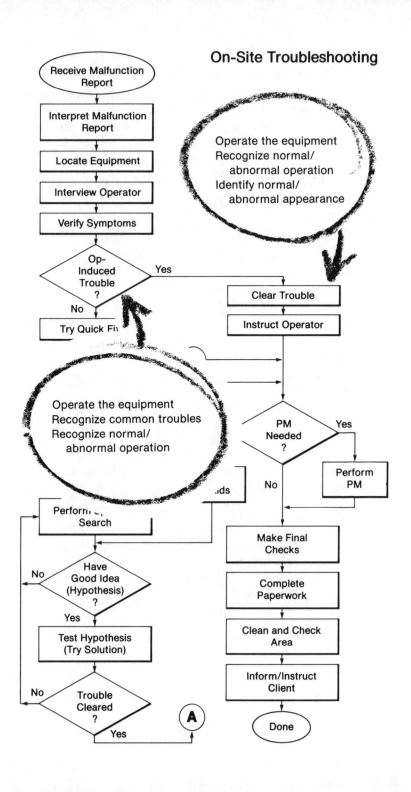

On-Site Troubleshooting

Receive Malfunction Report

Interpret Malfunction Report

Locate Equipment

Interview Operator

Verify Symptoms

Op-Induced Trouble ?

Operate the equipment
Recognize normal/
  abnormal operation
Identify normal/
  abnormal appearance

Yes

No

Try Quick Fix

Clear Trouble

Instruct Operator

Operate the equipment
Recognize common troubles
Recognize normal/
  abnormal operation

PM Needed ?

Yes

No

Perform PM

Perform Search

Have Good Idea (Hypothesis) ?

No

Yes

Test Hypothesis (Try Solution)

Trouble Cleared ?

No

Yes

Make Final Checks

Complete Paperwork

Clean and Check Area

Inform/Instruct Client

Done

A

Operator-Induced Trouble?

What leads you to the decision that an operator has left a control in an improper position, operated the equipment incorrectly, or caused the trouble to occur by poor maintenance? I think you would agree that at the very least, you would have to know what the controls do and the sequence in which they should be manipulated. If you think I'm being obvious again, why do most maintenance courses fail to insist that trainees learn to operate the equipment before moving into troubleshooting instruction?

What else? Common troubles. It helps to know the things that go wrong frequently, because many common troubles are operator induced.

And, there's something else. You need to be able to tell the difference between normal and abnormal operation, because operators sometimes report as a "trouble" a condition that is actually part of normal operation. They may not know the difference between normal and abnormal operation, but you have to. For example, that "funny sound" they report may be exactly correct and the "strange vibration" may be perfectly normal.

In the main, if troubleshooters can operate the equipment, recognize the difference between normal and abnormal operation, and can recognize the common troubles, they should be able to determine whether the trouble is operator induced. If you feel there is something else, list the skill beside this step of the task.

Clear Trouble

If the trouble is operator induced, what would trainee troubleshooters need to be able to do before they could practice clearing it? At the very least they need to be able to operate the system. They need to know what the controls do and what position they should be in. In addition, they need to be able to recognize the difference between normal and abnormal operation, so they can recognize the problem they have to clear. You can't clear 'em if you don't notice 'em.

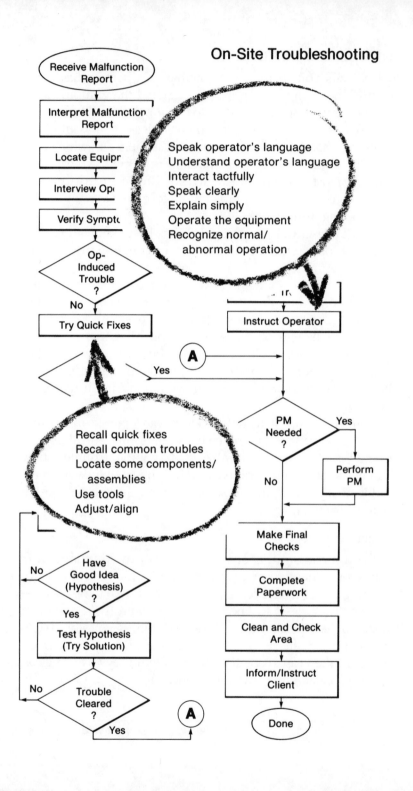

On-Site Troubleshooting

Receive Malfunction Report

Interpret Malfunction Report

Locate Equipr

Interview Op

Verify Sympt

Op- Induced Trouble ?

Speak operator's language
Understand operator's language
Interact tactfully
Speak clearly
Explain simply
Operate the equipment
Recognize normal/ abnormal operation

No

Try Quick Fixes

Instruct Operator

A — Yes

PM Needed ? — Yes

Perform PM

No

Recall quick fixes
Recall common troubles
Locate some components/ assemblies
Use tools
Adjust/align

Make Final Checks

Complete Paperwork

Clean and Check Area

Inform/Instruct Client

Have Good Idea (Hypothesis) ? — No

Yes

Test Hypothesis (Try Solution)

Trouble Cleared ? — No

Yes — A

Done

There may be another skill required here. The operator-induced trouble may be something other than an operational one — a power plug kicked out of its receptacle, a component bent or jammed, a pocket knife or a lipstick dropped into the works, a board not seated. Seems that troubleshooters need to recognize not just normal/abnormal appearance but also need to be able to spot things that appear where they don't belong.

Instruct Operator

To prevent future occurrences of operator-induced troubles, the operator should be told what the problem was and how it can be avoided. Of course, there are lots of ways that can be done, some of which are better than others.

"Look dummy, you keep dumping your phony fingernails into the works and you just may lose your fingers as well" somehow doesn't seem to be the best approach. And, "I can't believe you did that again" or "You keep wearing a tie in the machine shop and you'll lose your empty head" won't win friends and influence operators. Besides, comments like these don't tell anyone very much about how to avoid the problem tomorrow.

What would troubleshooters need to be able to do to instruct the operator? Clearly there needs to be an ability to speak and understand the operator's language. In addition, the troubleshooters will have to interact tactfully and not insult or humiliate the client. It's also helpful if they speak clearly and calmly and explain things simply.

Troubleshooters also need to be able to operate the equipment in order to demonstrate proper operation. And finally, they need to be able to recognize the difference between normal and abnormal operation so they can explain it.

Try Quick Fixes

If the trouble is not operator induced, the next step is to engage in rapid clearing actions. While verifying symptoms, or immediately thereafter, competent troubleshooters try one or more fast and easy solutions. If the machine is dead, they

---

quickly check to make sure it is plugged in. If there are interlock switches, they check to make sure they are actuated. If the car won't crank, they quickly check the battery *and* the battery terminals to make sure there is a good connection. What do they need to know to engage in these quick fixes? They need to know the troubles common to the equipment; which ones are quick and easy to cure, and how to cure them. Sometimes this means being able to carry out some adjustments and/or alignments and usually means being able to use some, but not all, tools. Remember that here we are only concerned with what it would take to carry out *this step* of the task. If you think about it a moment, you will see that it would be possible to assign someone the sole task of engaging in these rapid solutions. "OK, Charlie, we've got a symptom. Do your stuff." And you can imagine Charlie banging interlocked doors, jiggling wires, and changing light bulbs without knowing how to operate the system and without knowing how to recognize normal/abnormal operation.

Wait a minute, I hear you cry. Wouldn't Charlie have to know about safety precautions so that he could do his stuff without killing himself or the equipment? Good question. But if you think about that a bit more, you will see that "safety precautions" is not a skill. You don't tell people to use their safety precautions skill. You tell them to work safely, meaning to perform a task in one way—the safe way—rather than in some other way. Thus, people who perform tasks safely aren't performing different tasks from those who perform them dangerously; there is just a difference in the execution (Ooops!). So you are correct in saying that you would want Charlie to perform his rapid clearing actions safely. But rather than putting safety precautions in a skill list, you should include that item as part of the instruction in how to do correct (safe) clearing.

In some equipment a symptom can often be cleared by routine alignment or adjustment. If this is true for your equipment, add aligning and adjusting to your list of quick fix skills.

Competent troubleshooters may engage in quick fix actions at any time during the troubleshooting task. While checking the tension of a belt, for example, they may tighten the setscrew holding the pulley to the shaft. While preparing to check voltage at a test point, they may turn and push plugs into their sockets to make sure they are tightly seated. Efficient troubleshooters engage in rapid clearing actions because they know that the time involved is well worth the effort.

To carry out quick fixes, then, a troubleshooter must be able to recall quick fix actions and common troubles, locate some components on assemblies, use some tools, and possibly adjust and align.

On-Site Troubleshooting

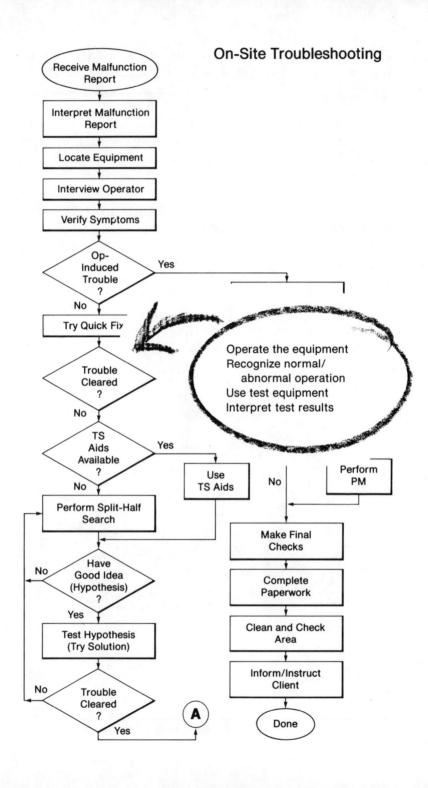

Trouble Cleared?

What does it take to decide this? Couldn't any idiot make such a simple decision? No. It's just not as simple as that. It requires being able to operate the system and recognize normal/abnormal operation. It might also require skill in using test equipment, torque wrenches, or gauges and in interpreting the results of the tests.

Troubleshooting Aids Available?

Here's an example of a task step that requires no prerequisite skill to perform. Sure, someone would have to know whether such aids are available, but that simply involves acquiring a piece of information rather than a skill. So suppose you were asked, "What would someone have to be able to do before being let into a course on how to decide whether troubleshooting aids are available?" I'm sure you would answer "Nothing." Correct, and so nothing is jotted beside this step in the task.

But the importance of a very simple task step is not related to the number of prerequisite skills required for its performance. It is rather important, for example, to replace the pin in a hand grenade before laying it down, even though the pin-replacing step is simple to perform and requires no previous skill to learn.

This point has important implications for training. Easy things to learn tend to get lost in the instructional shuffle just because they are easy, even though they are also of critical importance. Component location is a good example. It isn't difficult to teach people how to locate components, but since it is such a simple thing it often is left out of the instruction — resulting in graduates who can't do the job until they learn how to find what they are looking for. One instructor I talked to said, "I'd feel silly asking students to run around touching components as I called out their names." And yet it is still true that you can't fix 'em if you can't find 'em.

On-Site Troubleshooting

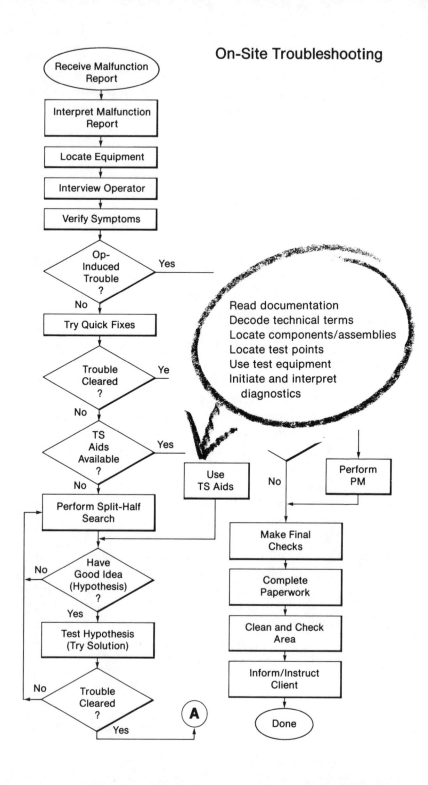

The other side of this issue is also worthy of mention; that is, there are times when something which is difficult to teach is of little or no importance. Let's consider a waveguide — a piece of pipe much like a piece of plumbing, used for transmission of ultrahigh frequency radio or radar signals. It has no moving parts, and the only thing that happens to it is that it gets bent out of shape or dented. The only fix is replacement. Yet I can recall a radar maintenance course whose instructors wanted to increase the four-hour block of instruction devoted to the *mathematics* of signals moving through a waveguide. The content was *totally irrelevant* to the needs of the trainees, but since it was difficult to learn, the instructors wanted more time to teach it. You must be constantly on the lookout for irrelevant instruction. Spot it with the results of the procedure you are currently practicing — use your list of skills derived from the troubleshooting task itself.

Use Troubleshooting Aids

Here is a task component that may consist of several steps in itself, and may vary widely in terms of the skills needed to implement it. On one end of the continuum is the simple If/Then troubleshooting aid listing symptoms in one column and suggested solutions in another. Users of these aids need to be able to read, interpret technical jargon, and locate the components/assemblies described. Possibly they would also need to be able to locate test points and use certain pieces of test equipment. For example, when the aid says something such as, "If the voltage at point A is less than 50 volts RMS, then turn pot 23 clockwise to increase voltage to 60 volts RMS."

On the other end of the continuum are the sophisticated troubleshooting aids, such as the diagnostics for locating computer malfunctions. Users of these must have at least the ability to operate the computer and interpret the special language on the video screen or printout when the diagnostic is run.

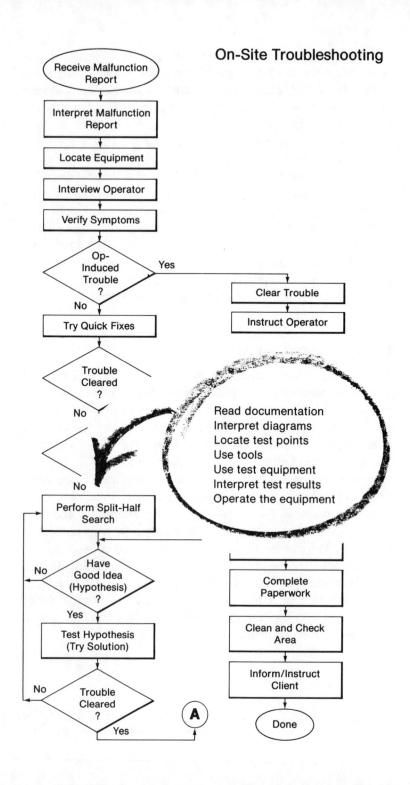

On-Site Troubleshooting

Receive Malfunction Report

Interpret Malfunction Report

Locate Equipment

Interview Operator

Verify Symptoms

Op-Induced Trouble ?

Yes → Clear Trouble → Instruct Operator

No

Try Quick Fixes

Trouble Cleared ?

No

No

Perform Split-Half Search

Read documentation
Interpret diagrams
Locate test points
Use tools
Use test equipment
Interpret test results
Operate the equipment

Have Good Idea (Hypothesis) ?

No

Yes

Test Hypothesis (Try Solution)

Trouble Cleared ?

No

Yes

A

Complete Paperwork

Clean and Check Area

Inform/Instruct Client

Done

Perform Split-Half Search

This is the systematic, point-by-point tracing of a trouble to its lair, which is used only after other sources of information have proven inadequate. It involves deciding which point to test, locating it, testing it, interpreting the results, and then decid-, ing, if necessary, which point to test next. So how do you answer the question, "What does someone need to be able to do to carry out a split-half search?" Use care and caution, as the tendency is to answer with a thoughtless "Everything!" That answer can lead to very expensive consequences.

In fact, troubleshooters need to know everything or close to it about a system *only* when there is inadequate documenta-tion (manuals, schematics, troubleshooting aids) available to aid them. If the documentation is complete and of high quality, troubleshooters don't need as much knowledge to do the job. If the documentation makes it easy to locate test points, then troubleshooters don't have to spend time memorizing them. If the documentation makes clear what is normal at each test point, then troubleshooters don't have to memorize that in-formation either. If the troubleshooting is done by an auto-matic routine, then troubleshooters have to know very little of the intricate details of the equipment.

Thus, how much troubleshooters have to know to com-plete a detailed split-half search is dependent on the com-pleteness, clarity, and usability of the documentation. If the documentation is properly constructed, then troubleshooters would need to be able to

- decode symbols on a diagram
- locate the component represented by a symbol on a diagram
- trace the signal or flow of the process on a diagram.

If the documentation is not properly constructed, then *in addition*, they may need to know how to do (memorize and do without assistance) any or all of the following:

- locate test points
- trace signal or flow from symptoms to malfunction

- interpret meter readings
- interpret waveforms
- determine test sequence.

Obviously then, the quality of documentation has implications for the length and content of troubleshooting courses.
When the manuals are poor, a course has to be longer to allow
more time for practice; and therefore, instruction is more
costly. The rule is: The poorer the manuals, the more practice
is required with them during the course so that trainees will
know how to use them when they head for the field. If any
documentation is merely handed to trainees on the last day of
the course, the chances are it will NOT be used on the job.

Would troubleshooters need any additional skills to complete a split-half search on your equipment? Would they need
to know how to use tools or test equipment? Assemble or
disassemble portions of the system? Operate the system? If so,
list these skills beside the split-half search step on your flowchart. Remember that you are listing the skills needed to
perform each step of your troubleshooting strategy and will
delete duplications later. So think about it again. Could someone complete a systematic split-half search for a trouble without knowing how to operate the equipment? Though it is a
costly mistake to graduate troubleshooters who do not know
how to operate the equipment, is the operating skill needed
for *this step* in the task? If so, note it. If not, don't.

Have Good Idea (Hypothesis)?

By this time experienced troubleshooters often feel they know
where the trouble is and either verify that their *knowing* is
correct and then clear the trouble, or they try a solution
directly. What does it take for them to decide that they have an
idea (hypothesis) worth testing? Careful, now. The question is
not about what it takes to locate a trouble, only what it takes to
decide whether a good hypothesis has been formed about
where the trouble is. Maybe it's easier to see if I ask it this way:
What would it take for you to decide whether you know how to

play a Bach fugue on the bassoon? Nothing more than recalling whether you had practiced bassooning that Bach piece and your level of skill in playing it.

Similarly, to decide whether a good hypothesis has been formed about where an equipment trouble is, you need only to recall whether your head is telling you, "In my opinion it's here rather than somewhere else because . . ."

What's that? You say it takes more than your opinion to tell whether a hypothesis is worth testing? Well, okay. But you don't have to shout. I just wanted to get your attention. You're right, of course. A good hypothesis is based on *information*; a guess by definition is based on *opinion* and is not a hypothesis.* Thus, a good hypothesis may be formed because prior testing has narrowed the search to a single component or unit, or because information (test results) collected so far has caused the troubleshooter to remember the trouble most likely to cause the symptoms.**

---

*Therefore, a "jump to conclusion" is at best a guess or a poor hypothesis based on little or no information.

**A course definition of *good hypothesis* may be influenced by company policy regarding spare parts or verification. When troubleshooters are well supplied with spares, they are often able to quickly test almost any hypothesis by simple substitution. If spares are sparse, or if company policy requires that trouble sources be verified before solutions are attempted, then a definition of a good hypothesis might be "a hypothesis that has been verified before a solution is attempted."

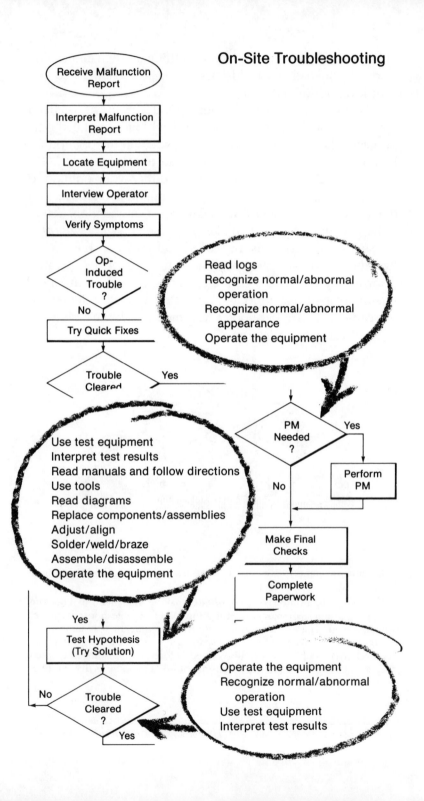

On-Site Troubleshooting

Receive Malfunction Report → **Interpret Malfunction Report** → **Locate Equipment** → **Interview Operator** → **Verify Symptoms** → **Op-Induced Trouble?**

Op-Induced Trouble? — No → **Try Quick Fixes** → **Trouble Cleared** — Yes →

- Read logs
- Recognize normal/abnormal operation
- Recognize normal/abnormal appearance
- Operate the equipment

PM Needed? — Yes → **Perform PM**

PM Needed? — No →

Make Final Checks → **Complete Paperwork**

- Use test equipment
- Interpret test results
- Read manuals and follow directions
- Use tools
- Read diagrams
- Replace components/assemblies
- Adjust/align
- Solder/weld/braze
- Assemble/disassemble
- Operate the equipment

Yes → **Test Hypothesis (Try Solution)** → **Trouble Cleared?**

Trouble Cleared? — No → Trouble Cleared? — Yes →

- Operate the equipment
- Recognize normal/abnormal operation
- Use test equipment
- Interpret test results

Test Hypothesis (Try Solution)

In some cases, a hypothesis is tested by verifying that the suspected culprit is guilty, often by use of test equipment or an adjustment manual and tools. In other cases a hypothesis is best tested by replacing the suspected component or subassembly because spares are readily available or because the only certain way to verify the cause is to attempt to clear the trouble.

Skills needed for hypothesis testing and trouble clearing may include adjusting and aligning, use of certain tools, and an ability to read and follow directions in the various manuals. Hypothesis testing may also require that troubleshooters be able to read and interpret diagrams and/or rig and operate test equipment. They also need to be able to determine whether test results mean that the section being tested is operating within tolerance, or whether an indication of abnormal operation is present.

To clear a suspected trouble your troubleshooters may need skills in addition to or instead of those shown above. They may need to be able to use a soldering iron or welding equipment, a winch or a hoist. Do they need to be able to operate the system to clear troubles? Whatever skills are required, write them beside this step on your flowchart.

Trouble Cleared?

You have already dealt with this step on page 78. Since the same skills apply, you can simply jot them down again on this flowchart. Moving right along . . .

Preventive Maintenance Needed?

Preventive maintenance (cleaning, oiling, readjusting, and occasional replacing of worn parts) not only increases the life of the equipment, it usually reduces the frequency of malfunctions and hence the cost of repair. Sometimes the decision to do preventive maintenance is made for troubleshooters by

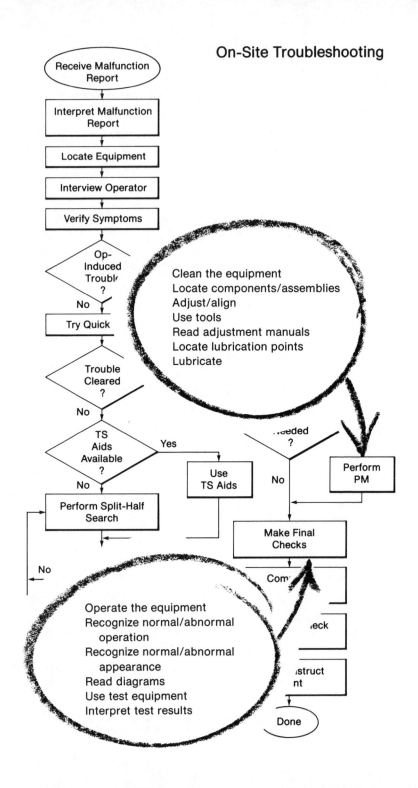

On-Site Troubleshooting

Receive Malfunction Report

Interpret Malfunction Report

Locate Equipment

Interview Operator

Verify Symptoms

Op-Induced Trouble?

No

Try Quick

Trouble Cleared?

No

TS Aids Available?

Yes → Use TS Aids

No

Perform Split-Half Search

Clean the equipment
Locate components/assemblies
Adjust/align
Use tools
Read adjustment manuals
Locate lubrication points
Lubricate

...eeded?

No

Perform PM

Make Final Checks

Com...

...eck

No

...struct
nt

Done

Operate the equipment
Recognize normal/abnormal
    operation
Recognize normal/abnormal
    appearance
Read diagrams
Use test equipment
Interpret test results

their organization: "Preventive maintenance will be performed each time the machine is serviced" or "PMs will be performed every six months." Often, however, this decision is left to the maintenance people themselves. What skills are needed to determine whether a PM is needed? If there is a log to read, then reading skill is required. If the decision is left to the troubleshooters, they will at least need the ability to recognize normal/abnormal operation and appearance and be able to operate the system.

Perform Preventive Maintenance

What skills do troubleshooters need to perform preventive maintenance procedures? It depends on the equipment, of course, but high on the list is an ability to clean a machine without damaging it or the troubleshooter, smudging up the machine's exterior, or messing up the area. This step often implies a need to be able to locate the items to be serviced. (In TV repair, cleaning is often done as a quick fix because spiders and wretched vermin are common causes of trouble.)

Troubleshooters will also need to be able to adjust or align, implying that they will also have to be able to use some tools and read and follow adjustment manuals. Some troubleshooters may need to lubricate at specific points; and if so, they also need to be able to find those points. If the documentation is poor or nonexistent, they may also have to be able to select the right lubricants and tools. Occasionally the PM procedure includes component replacement. When it does, troubleshooters need to be able to do this correctly.

Make Final Checks

When the trouble is cleared and the preventive maintenance has been performed, the competent troubleshooter checks the system to make certain it is operating as desired. Less competent people often fail to make final checks and sometimes leave a machine as badly off as when it was attacked or worse. Just recently I saw an example of this in the case of a recurring

On-Site Troubleshooting

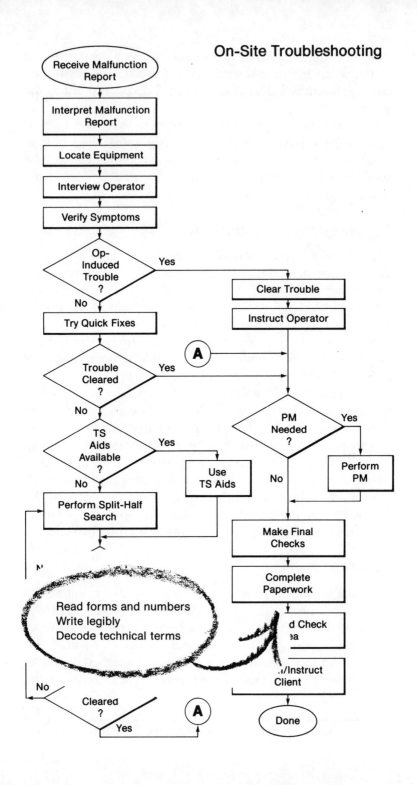

Receive Malfunction Report

Interpret Malfunction Report

Locate Equipment

Interview Operator

Verify Symptoms

Op-Induced Trouble ?
— Yes → Clear Trouble → Instruct Operator

No

Try Quick Fixes

Trouble Cleared ?
— Yes

No

A

TS Aids Available ?
— Yes → Use TS Aids

No

Perform Split-Half Search

PM Needed ?
— Yes → Perform PM

No

Make Final Checks

Complete Paperwork

Read forms and numbers
Write legibly
Decode technical terms

d Check
ea

/Instruct Client

No

Cleared ? — Yes

A

Done

trouble in an electronic typewriter. When the trouble popped up again recently we called our maintenance man, who then proceeded to clear that trouble in a spritely manner. But the machine still didn't work properly. Why? Nobody knew until the next day when a hotshot was brought to the scene. What *he* did was check all the parts of the machine he would handle if he were solving the original problem. The hotshot discovered that the less experienced man had failed to retighten a set-screw. Had the first troubleshooter checked his work, he might have found this oversight, saving time and client good will.

Performance of final checks requires ability to operate the system, discriminate between normal/abnormal operation and appearance, read diagrams, and use and interpret some test equipment.

Complete Paperwork

The world is full of paperwork and everyone, including the intelligent and productive, is caught in the web of forms, boxes, and bureaucracy. Kept-up records of repairs can be very useful to those who will troubleshoot the equipment in the future, of course, but often paperwork goes far beyond a simple required record of the repair and spares used. Some companies require the filling out of involved, elaborate forms that take a day or more to learn how to complete. What would trainees have to be able to do before practicing the completing of this documentation? Be able to read, of course, and write. In addition, they would have to be able to decode whatever technical terms may be on the forms. With those three prerequisite skills in place they would be ready to learn what and when to write in the boxes and what to do with the completed forms.*

---

*Form-filler-outers should be taught to use technical terms consistently, to aid in later malfunction analysis.

Completing paperwork is a step in the strategy that may seem trivial to you. It may be a nuisance, but it isn't trivial. Listen to a service rep in a large office equipment company. "One of our complaints with the instruction was that it didn't tell you about all the paperwork you need to do after fixing a problem. Then you get to the end of the course, and they hand you this big pile of paper. They gave us practice on the last day—a series of bugs just like a day in the field, and we had to do all the paperwork. But that wasn't enough practice in that part of it, and you look silly for the first week on the job."

Clean and Check Area

Company image is strongly influenced by employees who are in direct contact with clients. That means that telephone operators, salespeople, clerks, and maintenance people may have more impact on company image than all the rest of the employees combined. That's why telephone companies, for example, take great care to train their installers to clean up after themselves. They may be the best there is when it comes to installing and troubleshooting; but if they leave homes and offices cluttered with chips, shavings, pieces of wire, and sandwich bags, they do a lot of damage to their own and their company's image. Just a while ago I checked under the hood of a car I had ransomed from the dealer's repair shop and found a wrench, a rag, and an oil dipstick (not mine) lying across the top of the radiator. Guess how many times I've been back since.

"At a very young age," reported an experienced troubleshooter, "I got a job in a radio repair shop. On my first attempt, I quickly found a faulty tube, which I replaced, clearing the trouble. I was so happy I quickly delivered the set to the owner, along with the bill. I forgot (or I didn't know better) to dust out the back of the set. The next day the lady brought the set back and said we had charged her without fixing her radio. She pointed to the fact that there was dust all over most of the tubes. I've never fixed anything since then without cleaning it."

Are any skills needed before giving people practice in cleaning up after themselves? No, not usually. They just need to be told that cleaning up is part of the job and possibly be provided with a checklist that calls out this step, making it necessary for them to read the language. This is usually sufficient to train and remind troubleshooters not to annoy customers by leaving the area messy or strewn with tools or spare parts. (If they really want to make clients nervous, all they need do is leave a few old parts lying around. The clients will think the parts were left out of their machine when it was put back together.)

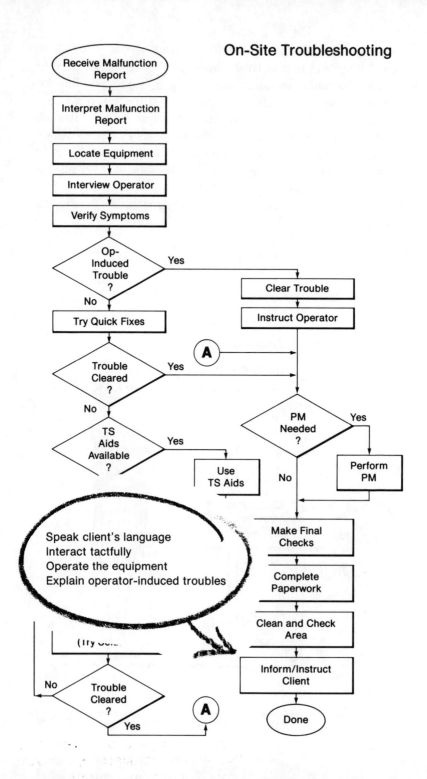

On-Site Troubleshooting

Inform/Instruct Client

As a last step, troubleshooters must inform the client that the equipment has been restored to service. This may be as simple as reporting, "It's OK now," but often it's a little trickier than that. Troubleshooters may need to tell the operator or someone else about how operation or preventive maintenance might be improved, or suggest that worn parts be replaced before they cause a malfunction. This needs to be accomplished without insulting or demeaning the client. "If ya weren't such a dummy, I wouldn't 've had to make this trip!" is usually not an acceptable form of communication.

To acomplish this final step successfully, then, troubleshooters need to be able to speak the language of their clients and to interact tactfully with them. They also need to know how to operate the equipment and be able to recall operator-induced troubles so they can explain how to avoid them in words the client will understand.

PUTTING IT TOGETHER

Now that you have derived skills from the troubleshooting strategy one step at a time, you can see what a skills list looks like. In the following two examples, the first list shows the skills that anyone must have to implement each step of the troubleshooting strategy, and the second shows the same list with the duplications removed.

List 1

Troubleshooting Step	Prerequisite Skills
Receive Malfunction Report	Read written language Interpret spoken language Decode technical terms

Troubleshooting Step	Prerequisite Skills
Locate Equipment	Recognize the equipment Read numerals? Read road map? Drive car? Climb poles? Pilot boat? Swim?
Interview Operator	Interact tactfully Speak operator's language Listen accurately and respond positively Decode technical terms Identify key comments Operate the equipment

Verify Symptoms	Operate the equipment
	Recognize normal/abnormal
	    operation
	Recognize normal/abnormal
	    appearance

Operator-Induced Trouble?	Operate the equipment Recognize common troubles Recognize normal/abnormal operation

Clear Operator-Induced
    Trouble
	Operate the equipment
	Recognize normal/abnormal
	    operation
	Recognize normal/abnormal
	    appearance

Troubleshooting Step	Prerequisite Skills
Try Quick Fixes	Recall quick fixes Recall common troubles Locate some components/ assemblies Use tools Adjust/align
Trouble Cleared?	Operate the equipment Recognize normal/abnormal operation Use test equipment Interpret test results
Use Troubleshooting Aids	Read documentation Decode technical terms Locate components/assemblies Locate test points Use test equipment Initiate and interpret diagnostics
Perform Split-Half Search	Read documentation Interpret diagrams Locate test points Use tools Use test equipment Interpret test results Operate the equipment

Troubleshooting Step	Prerequisite Skills
Test Hypothesis (Try Solution)	Use test equipment Interpret test results Read manuals and follow directions Use tools Read diagrams Replace components/assemblies Adjust/align Solder/weld/braze Assemble/disassemble Operate the equipment

The preceding part of the list itemizes the skills needed for the trouble-locating and -clearing portion of the strategy. Next come the skills needed for the remaining maintenance steps.

Maintenance Step	Prerequisite Skills
Instruct Operator	Speak operator's language Understand operator's language Interact tactfully Speak clearly Explain simply Operate the equipment Recognize normal/abnormal operation

Maintenance Step	Prerequisite Skills
Preventive Maintenance Needed?	Read logs Recognize normal/abnormal operation Recognize normal/abnormal appearance Operate the equipment
Perform Preventive Maintenance	Clean the equipment Locate components/assemblies Adjust/align Use tools Read adjustment manuals Locate lubrication points Lubricate
Make Final Checks	Operate the equipment Recognize normal/abnormal operation Recognize normal/abnormal appearance Read diagrams Use test equipment Interpret test results
Complete Paperwork	Read forms and numbers Write legibly Decode technical terms
Inform/Instruct Client	Speak client's language Interact tactfully Operate the equipment Explain operator-induced troubles

Competent troubleshooters may be required to have any or all of the preceding troubleshooting and maintenance skills, depending, of course, on the nature of their specific job descriptions and the equipment being serviced. When duplications are deleted from the list it looks like this:

List 2

Interpret spoken language	Recognize normal/abnormal
Read written language	appearance
Read Logs	Run diagnostics
Write the language	Check admustments
Interview operator	Recognize common troubles
Speak operator's/client's	Recall quick fixes
language	Complete paperwork
Interact tactfully	Use tools
Listen accurately	Adjust/align
Respond positively	Perform split-half search
Speak clearly	Use test equipment
Explain simply	Interpret test results
Identify key comments	Locate test points
Describe common troubles	Clean the equipment
Decode trouble reports	Lubricate
Decode technical terms	Locate lubrication points
Operate the equipment	Assemble/disassemble
Read documentation	Locate components/assemblies
Read adjustment manuals	Replace components/
Interpret diagrams	assemblies
Recognize the equipment	Solder/weld/braze
Recognize normal/abnormal	Read a map
operation	Drive a car

YOUR TURN

Now it's your turn to apply the skill-deriving procedure to your own troubleshooting strategy flowchart. You have two ways to go. Either you can set my skills list aside and derive your own, or you can lay my list beside your flowchart and modify it to fit your flowchart. But whichever option you choose, be specific. Rather than write "Use tools," as I did, name the tools. Rather than write "Use test equipment," name the test equipment. Name manuals that have to be read, diagrams that have to be interpreted, and forms that have to be filled out.

Here Is What To Do

1. Get out the flowchart you derived at the end of Chapter 3 and a pencil (no pens, please).
2. Consider the first step of the troubleshooting task on your flowchart and ask yourself, "What would someone need to be able to do to carry out this step?" That is, what skills would someone have to have to perform it? Remember, not every step will have prerequisite skills.
3. Write the skills beside the step on the flowchart.
4. Repeat the procedure for each step. Write all the skills needed; duplications will be deleted later.
5. Go back over the items you listed to make sure they are skills rather than subject matter. They're OK if you can put *can* in front of them and they still make sense. For example, "can adjust," or "can operate the system," are fine. On the other hand, "can electronic theory," is silly, telling you that you have listed subject matter rather than a skill.

   If you prefer, you can use the *Hey, Dad* test here. Instead of trying your items with just *can* in front of them, mentally preface each one like this: "Hey, Dad, let me show you how I can _____." If it has the ring of sense to it, you have written a skill. If not, you have listed a subject. For example, "Hey, Dad, let me show you how I can describe common troubles" sounds OK. But, "Hey, Dad, let me show you how I can algebra" doesn't grok. Delete it or list the skill that should be there instead.
6. Now delete the duplications and construct your master list of all the skills anyone would need to carry out the complete troubleshooting strategy on your flowchart.

The substance of your existing course can be compared with this list to determine whether (a) the correct content is included, (b) enough practice is given in key skills, and (c) learners are not required to "learn" skills they either already have or don't need while other requisite skills are left out.

NEXT?

There is another powerful tool called a skill hierarchy that can help you to test the appropriateness of your course content. In addition, it is useful for testing the sequence in which the instruction is presented.

The Skill
Hierarchy
(Freedoms and Constraints)

"I teach in a logical sequence" is an expression we have all heard instructors utter. And of course, it does make sense to teach in a logical rather than an illogical sequence. But let's think about that a bit. What is a logical sequence? Logical from whose point of view? The instructor's? The learner's? Is what is logical to one also logical to the other? And is teaching strategy good just because it's logical? Hmmm.

One problem with logical sequence is that there are several meanings attached to the expression, and one seldom knows which is meant without asking. One meaning, for example, is "chronological sequence." Here the instructor teaches first that which happens first; next, that which happens next; and so on.

In another meaning of logical sequence the instructor says, "I teach in a logical sequence, from the simple to the complex," and then begins teaching the most microscopic elements of the subject, moving toward the larger elements. In

Sequencing is often influenced by the degree of skill desired. For example, a study by Rigg and Gray[1] suggests that if trainees perform a skill correctly only once, the probability of performing it correctly a second time is only fifteen percent. If they are required to practice to the point where they can do it right three times in a row, the probability of doing it right the fourth time increases to fifty percent.

This doesn't hold true for all skills, of course; some require more or less practice to assure competence. But the point is a valid one; if you want to be sure that trainees can perform as desired when they leave you, sequence the instruction to insure that they receive repeated practice in the key skills.

---

[1] K. E. Rigg and B. B. Gray, *Estimating Skill Training and Retention Functions Through Instructional Model Analysis*, Periodic Report, Contract No. MDA 903-73-C-0278 (Monterey, Calif.: McFann, Gray and Associates, Inc., 1980).

electronics this usually means teaching about electrons in orbit first and then moving progressively through components and circuits and finally to systems. Unfortunately, what the learner means by "simple to complex" is exactly the opposite. The learner thinks of logical sequence as moving from the big picture to the big pieces of the big picture and then to the smaller pieces. In this sense the learner sees the instructor's sequence as illogical.

A third meaning of logical sequence is suggested by the nature of the equipment being taught. Instructors teach their way from one end of the equipment to the other, usually starting with content associated with the unit farthest to the left (or right) on the diagram, and then moving toward the other end. Although such a sequence of instruction may appear logical from the equipment's point of view, it may or may not be meaningful from the learner's point of view.

A SKILL HIERARCHY

How then should you sequence instruction? Given the varying nature of equipment and experience of trainees, what guidelines should you use? Successful sequencing guidelines respect the prerequisite relationships of the skills to be taught. This means that whenever the learning of a skill depends on having already learned another skill, the instruction will insist that learners first master the skill on which the other depends. If you had a map showing the prerequisite relationships between the skills being taught in your course, you could quickly tell whether those skills were effectively sequenced.

Such a map is called a skill hierarchy, and it is an extremely useful tool. Not only will it help you decide whether a course is teaching *all* the skills needed for competence, but it will also help you determine whether the sequence in which the learning occurs makes sense. More, it will show you how much leeway there is in the sequencing, show where the students might safely be given some freedom to decide their own sequence (sequence, not content) of instruction, and show where constraints on sequencing must be imposed. And if that isn't enough, a skill hierarchy will also help you see where you might make more efficient use of your limited instructional resources such as equipment, space, time, and instructors.

If you haven't already built a skill hierarchy, I think you will find it an interesting activity. All you need are some small pieces of paper or card stock about 2″ x 2″, two large pieces of paper, a pencil, rubber cement, and the list of skills you derived from your flowchart. What you are going to do is to arrange those skills on a piece of paper so that you can see the prerequisite relationships among them.

But first a description of the process.

RELATIONSHIPS

Suppose you had to learn (a) to type and (b) to take dictation. Could you learn either skill without knowing the other? You could, couldn't you? You don't need to know how to type to practice taking dictation, and you certainly don't have to know how to take dictation to learn how to type. We say, therefore, that the skills in this pair are independent of one another. They could be learned in either order.

Now suppose you had to learn (a) to type and (b) to read. Could you profitably practice reading without knowing how to type? You could, couldn't you? But what about the other way around? Could you profitably practice typing without knowing how to read? Doubtful. So, in this case, learning the typing skill depends on being able to read, and students should be taught to read before they are taught to type. Reading is a prerequisite skill to typing. There may be other prerequisite skills. That is, typing might be better learned if other skills are learned beforehand, too, but reading is at least one such skill.

When one skill is dependent on another, instruction should prevent students from studying them in the wrong, unprofitable order. Prerequisite skills should be sequenced and taught in prerequisite order, regardless of whether that order fits an instructor's style or preference, and regardless of what the students might prefer to learn first. Dependent skills impose a constraint on the instructional sequence and demand to be taught in a given order.

Independent skills, on the other hand, offer an area of freedom in sequencing. Since each such skill can be profitably learned even though others aren't known, it is possible to give the learners themselves the option of selecting the order in which they will study these skills.

A Picture Is Worth . . .

The skill hierarchy diagram depicts relationships between all the significant skills taught in a course. Anyone can see at a glance which skills are dependent on the mastery of others and which are not. Prerequisite skills are placed below those they support, and independent skills are placed beside one another. For example, (a) can type and (b) can take dictation would be shown in two boxes side by side.

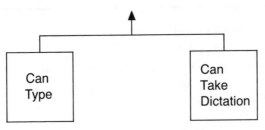

And, since typing depends on reading, these two skills would be shown this way.

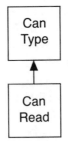

If you assume that reading skill is also prerequisite to being able to take dictation, we can show the three skills like this.

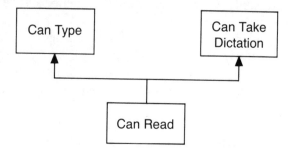

You read the hierarchy this way: "Students can learn to take dictation or to type in either order. Before they practice either of these skills, however, they need to be able to read." If you are thinking of one or more other skills that students would need before they practiced typing or dictation, you may want to practice adding them to this hierarchy.

Caution: Always keep in mind that a hierarchy is *not* intended to depict the steps in which a task is performed. Rather, it shows which skills must be in place before others may be profitably learned, and which can be learned without first learning others.

A Finer Line

The skills used in the example above are clearly dependent on or independent of one another and easy to place on a hierarchy. Sometimes it is harder to say whether one skill would have to be learned before another could be usefully practiced. Consider, for example, (a) disassemble the equipment and (b) replace components. Is it possible to learn one without knowing how to do the other? Of course, a troubleshooter might have to disassemble something before being able to get at the component to be replaced, but we are not concerned here with the sequence of steps in which the task is performed. We are concerned with the order in which the skills must be learned. If someone disassembled the equipment for me, I could practice replacing components. Similarly, I could practice disassembling without knowing how to replace components. So, I would consider these to be independent skills . . . but very closely related.

This is not as trivial an example as you might suppose. The replacement of electronic components in a fighter plane must often be preceded by several hours of disassembly of the armor to expose the innards. Those who do the disassembly don't have to know anything about electronics to learn how to do it, and the electronic techs could learn all about electronics without ever learning how to disassemble the armor.

FREE SAMPLE

On the last page of this book you will find a complete hierarchy that I derived from the skills listed at the end of Chapter 4 (page 100). Not only will it give you a model to work with, but also it should make you feel better when you discover that most of the skills you will put into your hierarchy are independent of one another—they can be learned in any order. It almost always works out this way, for almost every subject area. The competent performer has to have a lot of competence, but the subject matter itself imposes few constraints on the order in which the skills must be taught.

Read the hierarchy from top to bottom (even though the arrows point up). For example, on the left side of the hierarchy, locate the box that says, "complete preventive maintenance." Read down that part of the hierarchy this way: Before people can do a PM they need to know how to (a) complete the paperwork, (b) clean the equipment, and (c) adjust/align the system. These three skills can be learned in any order. But before people can practice adjusting and aligning they need to know how to (a) operate the equipment, (b) read adjustment

NOTE FOR THE CURIOUS

As you read the "clear trouble" and "locate trouble" portions of the hierarchy, you may wonder why "adjust/align system" is listed under trouble clearing and not under trouble locating. After all, when you adjust or align, you learn something about where the trouble is or is not. Some troubleshooters suggest completing adjustment and alignment procedures early in the troubleshooting sequence for this very reason.

Here's why it is shown where it is. *Every* time you try to clear a trouble you learn something about where the trouble is or is not, depending on whether the clearing action succeeds or fails. Nonetheless, trouble clearing actions are different from trouble locating actions. Actions such as adjusting and aligning, for example, are intended to clear troubles directly; they are not analytical actions intended to locate troubles. If adjustment or alignment clears the trouble, that's the end of it. If it doesn't, you keep hunting. On the other hand, trouble-locating actions, such as reading a meter, must always still be followed by trouble-clearing actions. Thus:

- Trouble-*locating* actions are intended to tell you something about where a trouble is so that you can *then* try a clearing action.
- Trouble-*clearing* actions are intended to eliminate troubles directly, even though they also tell you something about where the trouble is or isn't.

That's why "adjust/align system" and "replace components/assemblies" are shown as skills needed for clearing and not for locating.

This may be a lot more than you wanted to know about the distinction; but since the issue was raised during the testing of the book, it seemed worth exploring . . . at least a little.

manuals, and (c) use tools. Again these three skills can be learned in any order. And so on. . . . (Note that "read the language" and "write the language" are shown as subordinate to the skill, "complete paperwork." This may seem trivial only until you work with people who don't have these skills.)

Here is something interesting to note, which has important implications for the management of maintenance programs. The skills listed under "clear trouble" and "locate trouble" don't overlap very much. People who clear troubles don't have to know how to do most of what the trouble locators have to do and vice versa.

But also note that what trouble locators have to be able to do requires more time to learn. Does that suggest that it is highly inefficient to expect all maintenance personnel to be able to locate as well as repair? Or might it be more efficient to concentrate on teaching most of them only how to locate the common troubles and leave the rest of the locating to a cadre of hotshots? And to make hotshots out of only those trouble clearers who show aptitude for it? The correct answers to these questions can cost or save your organization millions of dollars.

YOUR TURN

Now that you have studied the procedure and devoured the free sample, it's your turn to create a hierarchy showing the relationships of the skills on your list. I must forewarn you, though, that two strange things may happen as you do so. First, you may find yourself adding skills that weren't there before. When you start saying, "Before they can practice doing *this* they need to be able to _____," you may discover that there are more prerequisite skills than those you wrote on your list. Second, you may discover that what you wrote down as a skill is really a description of subject matter or content that should be deleted. Yes, the business of drafting skill hierarchies is a very useful one, indeed.

And, you may disagree with some of the placements of skills on my sample hierarchy (how dare you!). Although you may be correct, the only way to know for sure would be to write your own detailed descriptions of the skills (called objectives). It is not useful to try to generate hierarchies in the abstract, because it becomes impossible to determine which skills are subordinate to others unless you tie them to specific equipment and circumstances.[1] Therefore, rather than spend time trying to correct my hierarchy, use it as a generalized model from which to construct your own.

Here Is What to Do

1. Find two large sheets of paper, a pencil (pens won't do for this activity), some 3″ by 5″ cards or a pad of 3M Post-it® Notes (1-1/2″ by 2″), and an eraser. If you use cards, you will need scissors as well as rubber cement. Cut the cards into pieces about 2″ by 2″. (Aren't you glad you had all that cutting and pasting practice in kindergarten? Didn't realize how useful it would be, did you?)

2. Work *across* the longer dimension of your paper. At the top write a description (call it a terminal objective if you know what those are) of what your troubleshooters should be able to do when competent at the troubleshooting task as that task is defined in your environment. List the items that troubleshooters will have available on the job, such as tools, test equipment, and manuals. Write what troubleshooters are expected to do, and how well they have to do it to be considered competent. Also, name the specific equipment that is the object of the maintenance, so that anyone reading the hierarchy will be able to compare the skills shown there with the equipment and the ultimate purpose of those skills.

3. Using the list of skills you derived from your flowchart,

---

[1] If you want to sharpen your hierarchy-deriving skill beyond what this chapter will allow, you need to be able to prepare instructional objectives. For help, read R. F. Mager, *Preparing Instructional Objectives*, 2nd ed. (Belmont, Calif.: Pitman Learning, Inc., 1975).

write the name of each skill on one of your cards or note slips.

4. Place all the skills in front of you and start to review them a pair at a time — it doesn't matter where you start. Pair by pair, ask yourself if one skill could be learned if the other were unmastered and vice versa. "Could someone learn *this* skill without being able to do *that* one?" And conversely. If the answer to both questions is yes, they will be placed side by side on your hierarchy. If one skill depends on the other, the one that has to be learned first should be placed below the other on the hierarchy.

5. When you begin to see the pattern of how the skills will all hang together, place them on the large sheet of paper and move them around until you have depicted all the skill relationships. Stick them down — they can be easily unstuck and moved again.

6. Draw pencil lines between the skills to show relationships and modify as needed. Refer to my sample hierarchy to see how these lines might be drawn.

At this stage, if some relationships are still difficult to depict, refer to the course objectives. If there are no objectives, you will have to solve the problem by writing a brief description of each skill. For example, if the skill is "adjust servos," briefly describe the adjustment to be made and the tools and test equipment that will be used. With a clearer picture of the dimensions of the skill, you should be able to resolve questions about where it belongs on the hierarchy.

7. Test your hierarchy by reviewing the relationship between each pair of skills. Look at a dependent pair (a pair connected by a line) and answer the question, "Is it true that this (lower) skill must be learned before this (upper) one can be learned?" For the independent skills, answer this question, "Is it true that either of these skills could be learned without knowing how to do the other?"

For each skill, ask yourself whether all of the subordinate skills are on your hierarchy. If not, add them. For example, for

TROUBLESHOOT YOUR HIERARCHY

There is a "common trouble" that many people experience the first time or two they build a skill hierarchy, a trouble that oozes out of their ability to draw flowcharts. They tend to draw the hierarchy as though it were a flowchart, confusing the sequence of steps followed in performing a task with the *skills* needed to perform those steps. Their hierarchy tends to show what is done first, second, and so on in the performance of a task, rather than showing which skills have to be learned before other skills can be profitably practiced.

Here's how to avoid this trap.

- First, make sure that each item on the hierarchy can be preceded by the word *can*; that will help guarantee that you are describing skills rather than content. "Can adjust" and "can perform PM" talk about skills. On the other hand, "can basic electronics" and "can theory of operation" don't make sense, telling you that you have put subject matter on your hierarchy rather than skills.
- Second, think of the hierarchy as an organization chart where higher level things appear nearer the top and lower level things appear nearer the bottom. Then when checking any skill on the hierarchy say to yourself, "Never mind the sequence of steps in which this task is performed; what, if anything, must someone have to be able to do before I would let them practice this skill?"

the skill "complete forms," name the forms and then ask yourself whether the hierarchy shows "read the language" and "write the language" as subskills. If not, add them. (If your forms can be completed by making Xs, your troubleshooters won't need to be able to write the language before practicing form filling.)

8. When all pairs of skills pass your inspection, draw the entire hierarchy onto a clean piece of paper. Keep it in pencil, as you may want to make changes when you ask your colleagues to review it.

With heirarchy in hand you will have another tool for checking the content and instructional sequencing of your troubleshooting course; that is, you will be able to make sure that the skills needed to perform the troubleshooting task are actually being taught, and that unnecessary content is excluded. Further, you will be able to determine whether or not the sequence in which the skills are now being taught conforms to the constraints shown on the hierarchy. Next, you will be able to check for ways to improve the efficiency of allocating course resources. It is possible that the hierarchy will suggest ways to increase individual practice through increased use of existing training equipment. And finally, perhaps it will suggest how inefficient training designed around a lecture-in-the-morning, lab-in-the-afternoon format can be replaced by instructional policies that are more learner oriented.

NEXT?

It is time now to turn to the instructional practices and procedures through which competence is developed and skills are sharpened. Given a picture of the instructional state of the art and a model of an ideal troubleshooting course, you will be able to compare actual instructional practices with desirable ones and spot further opportunities for improving your course design and delivery system.

PART ◇ 3

Instructional Practice

The Instructional State of the Art
(The Bridge to Competence)

Just as a beautifully designed piece of machinery can be abused by its users, a well-designed course can be mangled by its implementers (instructors). On the other side of the coin, just as poorly designed equipment can sometimes be made to sing in the hands of the competent, poorly designed courses can sometimes be made to work when implemented by highly skilled instructors. Further, just as the environment in which a machine is used can have an effect on how well it works and how long it will stay working, the environment in which instruction is offered can have an effect on how well the instruction succeeds.

When tweaking a troubleshooting course, therefore, it is important to assess the implementation of instruction — the environment in which instruction is offered and the instructional practices and procedures being used. Implementation includes everything about instruction that impinges on learners, such as the comfort or discomfort of the chairs and the visibility and clarity of information presented by lecture, book, or film. It also has to do with the sequence in which the information is presented and with rules about how and when to practice. It has to do with the conditions under which the trainees are living and with the mood communicated by the instructors. Implementation, in short, has to do with the *operation* of a course, and it can make or break a course as surely as an operator can make or break a piece of hardware. To remind yourself of some common errors of implementation, think back to courses you have had. What turned you on? What turned you off? What made you want to keep going? What made you want to give up?

The purpose of this chapter, then, is to provide you with tools for checking out the implementation of your course — tools with which to compare what IS happening now with what OUGHT TO BE happening in a course implemented at or near the state of the art. Although there are any number of subtle course operation details that you might spot and improve, this chapter points up only the more common and costly obstacles to effective, efficient course operation and potential competence on the job.

ANOTHER BLACK BOX?

Don't let anyone convince you that you can't spot troubles in course operation without being an expert in course design and implementation. It isn't true. You don't have to be a chicken to sort eggs, and you don't have to be a mechanical engineer to know that your car isn't working because a wheel fell off.

Several years ago, two missile maintenance friends of mine decided to verify their suspicion about just how much theory and other knowledge was needed before one could do something useful in missile maintenance. So, they tried an interesting instructional experiment. One night these officers took their wives to the radar park where they taught them how to safely attach a single piece of test equipment in the form of a black box to the radar system and to interpret the major readings. In just two hours the women were able to determine whether the radar was operational and, if so, how well it was working. They didn't know anything about electrons in orbit or resistances or radar. But they knew how to tell whether and how well the system was working . . . with only two hours of instruction.

Then another interesting thing happened. During a visit, the general in charge of the West Coast Air Defense Command heard about the experiment and said to the two young officers, "I want you to teach me how to do that." They did. And the general went back to headquarters with the little black box tucked under his arm.

One dark night he traveled from site to site testing the operational readiness of the weapons under his command, to the astonishment of the electronically trained commanders. For then there was hell to pay. Many of the systems weren't operating as well as they were reported to be. Though the general didn't know how to build a missile system, and though he didn't know how to operate or repair one, he sure could tell whether one was or was not operating up to snuff.

The Mini-Plot

To spot the major obstacles to instructional effectiveness and efficiency, your black box will take the form of a checklist of things to look for and questions to ask. You'll find it in Chapter 9. With the tools you prepared earlier (you *did*, didn't you?) already available, only a little more preparation is in order before you're ready to use the checklist.

First, because instruction doesn't work merely because someone says it does, it will be useful to review the *purpose of instruction* and the *major characteristics of instruction with the power to teach*. Then, to help develop a picture of what OUGHT TO BE, there will be a *summary of the major characteristics of the instructional state of the art*, with an illustration of what each looks like when present. Then, in Chapter 7, you will find a description of a model course, a composite of the features you would expect to see in a troubleshooting course operating at or near the state of the art. Finally, Chapter 8 will list and describe the common troubles found in course implementation.

With that preparation you should be ready to apply the Chapter 9 checklist to your own course.

THE PURPOSE OF INSTRUCTION

Why bother to instruct? Why bother to take the time and effort to construct those units of activity called courses? The correct answer is that we do it because one or more people cannot now perform something they need to be able to perform as you and others want them to perform it. If they were already in the shape you wanted them, there would be no need to instruct. For example, consider this dialogue:

> *Teach: Now I'm going to teach you how to walk.*
> *Stu: Wait a minnit! I already know how to walk!*
> *Teach: Don't try to get ahead of the class.*
> *Stu: But I don't need your instruction on walking.*
> *Teach: If you don't have my instruction you'll never*
> *pass my test.*

You see the point. Instruction that isn't needed isn't any good, no matter how colorful the slides or how eloquent the lectures.

The precise purpose of instruction is to facilitate learning . . . and learning means change. Instruction that doesn't change anyone has no instructional value. To have maximum value, instruction must change each trainee as efficiently as the state of the art will allow. It is not the purpose of instruction to simply continue until a set time period comes to an end. Nor is it the purpose to use students as an audience for instructors. The purpose of instruction is to facilitate the development of the competence needed by *each trainee*, as efficiently and as humanely as possible.

Instructional Power

Instruction with the most power (most bang for the buck)

    a. changes people
      b. in desired directions
        c. without undesired side effects
          d. in the least time
            e. at the least cost.

An exploration of each of these components of instructional power will help you to derive the ideal characteristics of instruction.

A. Changes People

Instruction that doesn't change people is powerless, just like medicine that has no effect. If the learners can't be shown to be different in their competence when the instruction is completed, it was of no value to them. Therefore, the only test of whether instruction works is the test of student performance, not instructor performance.

In a little book on ventriloquism[1] there is an interesting example of a *non*instruction. It is attempting to tell how to make a distant voice, the voice that appears to come from a suitcase or from behind a curtain rather than from the figure itself (ventriloquists don't call them dummies). The entire instruction reads as follow:

> You screw up the vocal cords and throw the voice backwards, trying, as it were, to make the sound strike the back of your head.

There. You've had the course, so let's see you do it. You say you can't? Maybe you weren't paying attention; maybe there's something wrong with your motivation. Better read the instruction again. There! Now can you do it? Mmmm. Maybe

---

[1]Fred T. Darvill, *How to Become a Ventriloquist* (San Francisco: Fred Darvill, 1937), p. 12.

---

you'd better sign up for a course in note taking or good study habits. Or maybe you need one on improving self-awareness.

You see the point. It doesn't matter how expressive or colorful or dedicated the instructor is, if the student isn't changed by the instruction it didn't work . . . it was powerless.

B. In Desired Directions

Mere change isn't good enough. Instruction needs to change people in the direction of its purpose. If instruction exists to facilitate change toward desired competence, the instruction with the most power is the one that most efficiently moves each trainee from existing competence to desired competence. For some trainees this means a great deal of change (lots of learning needed), and for others it means only a little. Of course, if trainees can already perform as desired, then no instruction is needed . . . if they ain't broke, don't fix 'em.

C. Without Undesired Side Effects

Have you ever cleared a trouble only to discover that, somewhere along the line, you put another one in? Welcome to the club. Instruction can be like that. It can teach people what they need to know and, at the same time, stomp all over their motivation to learn more. It can send them away feeling less good about themselves, less interested in learning, less interested in the job or the company, and hostile toward the instructors. If after taking a course, you have said, "I hope I never hear of that subject again" or "I've never been so humiliated in my life" or "I'll never take a course from that instructor again," you have experienced exactly the sort of unwanted side effects we are talking about. Instruction with maximum power achieves its results without such unwanted side effects.

D. In the Least Time

The practice of continuing instruction after the desired learning has been achieved (the instructional objectives have been accomplished) is just as questionable as the practice of selling pills to people who have been cured of their problems. Instruction that lasts longer than is needed is wasteful of materials and time. It is also wasteful of student motivation (who among us is highly enthusiastic about having to learn what we already know?). Therefore, instruction with maximum power continues until the desired results are achieved for each learner, and then it stops.

E. At the Least Cost

Watch a child writing with fist curled around the pencil, tongue out, legs wrapped around the chair, and all muscles tensed. Then watch an adult write with a flowing hand, and you will see the elegance of economy of motion. Watch the difference between a duffer and a pro on the golf course or a novice dancer and a ballerina. You will see the difference between something implemented with awkwardness and tension, and something achieved with elegance and grace.

Instruction, too, can be implemented awkwardly rather than elegantly. It can include embellishments of content or instructional hardware that aren't related to the purpose of that instruction; for example, video programs complete with music and lots of titles that have nothing to do with the objectives at hand. It can overwhelm students with busywork. More, it can stand in their way because equipment isn't immediately available or doesn't work. It can delay them with "mediated" lessons that aren't needed or "computerated" practice that doesn't facilitate achievement of objectives.

No, elegance in instruction doesn't mean fancy; it means smooth, to the point, and economical. So, instruction functioning at or near the state of the art avoids unnecessary, and therefore costly, practices—and uses materials, equipment, and procedures that will get the job done most directly. It strives for the elegance of least motion, rather than embellishment for its own sake.

THE INSTRUCTIONAL STATE OF THE ART

When the best available techniques and procedures are used to change people in desired directions without undesired side effects in the least time and at the least cost, instruction is said to be functioning at the state of the art; that is, as well as it can. As with other disciplines, the edges of the instructional art are a little fuzzy and sometimes elusive. No matter. The characteristics of primary importance are clear enough for all to see. We will briefly explore each of them along with their implications for course operation. This composite picture of normal operation will provide the standard against which actual course characteristics can be compared.

But if the next few pages describe a form of instruction that is strange to you, read Chapter 7 before proceeding.

1. Instruction exists only where it is a solution or remedy for a problem in human performance.

People who are not doing what they are supposed to do are not necessarily in need of training. They may not be performing as desired because they are punished for desired performance; or there may be genuine obstacles to desired performance, such as lack of tools or authority; or they may never have been told exactly what is expected of them. Among the number of remedies for such problems, instruction should be used only when it is the most efficient solution.

Selection of the best remedy must be based on an analysis of the job situation that compares discrepancies between what people *are* doing, and what they *should be* doing. Then it ferrets out the reasons for the discrepancies and points to solutions. The analysis[2] should be carried out as soon as someone says training is needed — just to assure that a course isn't constructed on false premises.

---

[2]See R. F. Mager and Peter Pipe, *Analyzing Performance Problems* (Belmont, Calif.: Pitman Learning, Inc., 1970).

2. Instructional objectives have been derived from competent performance on the job.

To guarantee that the purposes of the instruction match the needs of the job, it is necessary to derive the outcomes of the instruction from the same needs; that is, from the job itself. Job-derived objectives are the key to insuring that the content of instruction will facilitate development of the actual skills needed on the job.

Instructional developers do this by following a procedure very much like the one you have experienced on your way through this book. First they make competent performance visible either by flowchart or some other method. Then they derive the skills that anyone would need to perform the tasks competently. After that they draft objectives describing the limits or boundaries of each of the skills and construct a hierarchy. Just like you have done.

3. Each student studies and practices only those competencies not yet mastered to the level described by the objectives.

Students differ in the skills they bring to a course; so, a course that makes all of them spend the same amount of time studying the same things is inefficient and mangles their motivation. The efficient course bases the selection of what to study and how long to study on what the individual student can do. Students study only those things they cannot yet do to the satisfaction of the objectives.

They choose the next unit of instruction they will attempt on the basis of completed prerequisites. The student reads the objective of a new unit and then decides if he or she can already perform as the objective demands. If not, then the unit is studied and the skill practiced. If so, then the criterion test associated with the objective is asked for and completed as required. If the performance matches or exceeds the criteria called for in the objective, the student is encouraged to move ahead to the next unit. If it does not, an instructor diagnoses

Course Map

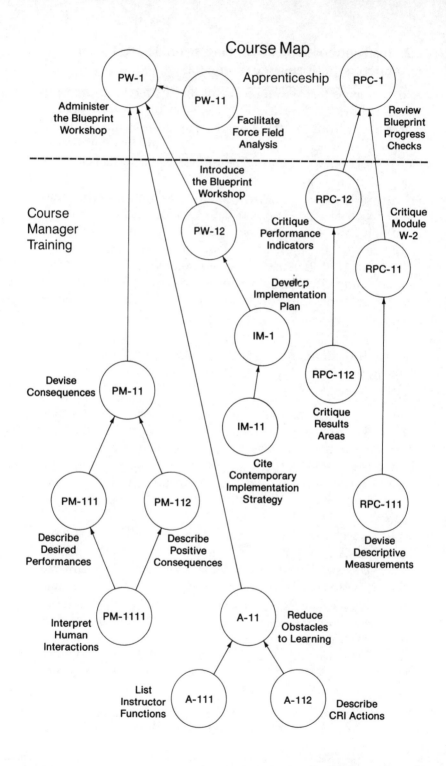

the problem and prescribes a remedy, such as additional practice or another explanation or demonstration. But there is no punishment or stigma attached to a trainee's trying a criterion test and not yet being competent. (Chapter 7 describes the procedure in more detail.)

This procedure can be implemented only if the following components have been prepared in advance:

- instructional objectives clearly describing the desired competencies and the criteria by which competence will be measured
- measuring instruments (called criterion tests or performance checks) for assessing competence
- a course map[3] or similar device showing trainees all the units of the course and how they relate (The course map is derived mainly from the hierarchy and shows which units a trainee may work on at each point in the course.)
- a course rule informing trainees of procedure, such as, "Study only those modules for which you have completed all prerequisites."

4. Students' progress is controlled by their own competence.

If the purpose of the course is to develop competence, there is little sense in forcing students to complete a course faster than their competence will allow. It is also wasteful to require that trainees remain in a course environment after they have de-

---

[3] Page 128 shows an example of a course map taken from a management development course. Students begin at the bottom and work their way upward. Circles represent units of instruction developed around skills, rather than around content. Arrows show which modules must be completed before others are studied; for example, PM-111 and PM-112 must be mastered before PM-11 is studied, while A-111 and A-112 may be studied in either order. The course map is reprinted by permission from Bonnie MacLean Abney, "Blueprint for MBO Course Manager's Certification Program" (San Mateo, Calif.: Abney & Associates).

veloped the competence prescribed by the objectives. The efficient course, therefore, encourages students to move ahead only as rapidly as their competence permits. Such a practice assures that each skill building block is in place before the next is added.

Implementation of this procedure requires measuring instruments (criterion tests, performance checks) and three course rules.

- Trainees are expected to study and practice until they can perform as desired.
- Trainees may demonstrate their competence on a unit of instruction by taking the criterion test when they feel ready to do so.
- Trainees may challenge the criterion tests without study if, after reading the objective, they are confident of their ability.

If there are equipment constraints, one or two more rules may be needed to handle the scheduling of equipment use.

5. Instruction is directly related to accomplishment of the objectives.

Although equipment may have redundant or backup circuits, it seldom has circuits or components that don't have anything to do with the purpose of the machine. Similarly, instruction consists of what is needed to accomplish the objectives. Given that the purpose of instruction is to facilitate the development of competence, the most efficient course is the one that has the least waste motion. This does not mean that not a single word or ounce of energy can be directed at activities or topics not directly related to course outcomes; it does mean that instructional fat is kept at a minimum.

Instructional relevance is accomplished through the design of the instruction, helped by one or more additional course rules. For example, "Study alternate resources only if you feel the main resource to be inadequate." In addition the instructors have to be taught how to function in such a learning environment—as coaches who help individual students as needed rather than as performers who dispense the same information to all whether needed or not.

6. Instructional materials impose a minimum of obstacles between the learners and the learning.

Instructional materials can be relevant to objectives and at the same time be nearly unusable. They can be hard to read and understand, incomplete, and even insulting. They can require more page flipping than necessary, and waste trainees' time with waiting to obtain and operate irrelevant instructional hardware. Trainees may be required to view an entire film when only a short segment is pertinent, and they may be further frustrated by the obstacle of long musical introductions to films and videotapes.

Conversely, the elegant course is designed to minimize the obstacles between the learner and the learning. This characteristic is also enhanced by methods of course implementation. During course development, instruction and implementation are tested and revised until obstacles are identified and removed. Needed equipment and materials are immediately available to instructors and students alike. Course rules make it clear that students are free to use materials, written or audiovisual, when they are ready to do so. And instructors don't impose rules unrelated to the purpose of the course.

7. Instruction is presented through the simplest delivery mechanisms consistent with the objectives, the learners, and the learning environment.

Least cost is realized, in part, by refraining from "shooting flies with an elephant gun," by using those instructional media that most directly accomplish the objectives and that are consistent with the characteristics of the students. Thus, elaborate videotape programs are not produced when a few pieces of paper will do the job more directly, and a classroom lecture is not presented when the same information can be more efficiently given by videotape or slides and audiocassette.

This characteristic is developed during instructional design. Designers review each objective and determine what things and space will be needed to allow students to practice the substance of the objective. Then they determine which delivery mechanisms will teach them what they need to know before they practice the objective. Finally, they select among the available, qualified possibilities those that are easiest for students to use and most economical. Thus, the media through which the instruction is presented are selected on the basis of the objectives to be accomplished, rather than instructor preference or student desires.

8. Students are provided with an opportunity to practice each objective and to obtain feedback regarding the quality of their performance.

Doing or practicing what the objectives describe is the surest way to competence. To be effective, however, the practice must be accompanied by feedback: information that tells trainees about the quality of the practice. Without the feedback, performance might not improve. So, state-of-the-art instruction always makes practice and feedback in each key skill available, even though not all learners will need to study each skill.

Relevant practice with feedback is a characteristic insured by good course design. For each objective, designers derive what students will need to do to practice the objective, and the method by which immediate feedback will be presented. Then they write that practice with feedback into each instructional unit, assuring its availability for each important skill or competence included in the course.

9. Learners receive repeated practice in skills that are used often or are difficult to learn.

Practicing a skill once is a great deal better than not having practiced it at all. The more a skill is practiced, however, the more likely it is to be available and used automatically when needed. People forget things, and they tend to forget fastest the things they have practiced least. Therefore, the state-of-the-art course is sequenced so that wherever possible the skill learned today is practiced as part of the skill learned tomorrow.

Implementation of this desired characteristic is accomplished mainly through use of a course map (page 128) derived from the skill hierarchy. Training begins with the lowest level skills at the bottom of the map. Each time they practice the skills to which those low level skills are prerequisites, trainees reinforce earlier learning.

Application of the repeated practice principle has special implications for the troubleshooting course. Care is always taken to make sure that learners are able to operate the equipment they will be troubleshooting. The troubleshooting course almost always begins with operator training, except where trainees are cross-training from one kind of equipment to a similar kind. Care is also taken to insure that every learner is able to quickly locate (put a finger on) each component or assembly he or she will be expected to find on the job. (You can't fix 'em if you can't find 'em.) Practice with test equipment begins early and continues throughout the course, as does practice with the documentation that will be used on the job. The poorer the documentation, the more practice trainees should receive with it during the course. Finally, since operator-induced troubles are so commonly encountered, learners should be regularly faced with such problems during training.

10. Learners receive immediate feedback regarding the quality of their test performance.

If the purpose of instruction is to develop competence as efficiently as possible, then the delay of test feedback imposes an obstacle to student progress. For optimal progress, competence must be checked out as soon as it is demonstrated by completion of a criterion test. Delay in feedback holds back student progress. In addition, it prevents students from receiving the reward associated with a job well done.

Immediate feedback is accomplished with a course rule to the effect that an instructor will check trainees' performance as soon as they have completed a criterion test. (When procedure is being checked, for example, when a student is demonstrating the skill of disassembly, the instructor assesses the process as well as the outcome.) In addition, instructors must be trained to make themselves available as soon as possible to those who are demonstrating their competence.

11. Desired student performances are followed by consequences they consider favorable.

People learn to avoid the things they are hit with. If students perform as desired and then find themselves punished, humiliated, insulted, or demeaned, they will be less likely to perform as desired again. To maintain and increase motivation requires that when students do the things expected of them, their world gets a little brighter, not dimmer. While this does not mean that each desired performance must be followed by a tangible reward, it does mean that at the very least

- the desired performance must be recognized, and
- not be followed by an unpleasant event or remark. ("So you finally finished that right did you?" isn't going to make any trainee feel confident.)

It also means that room is made for making errors during learning; and though mistakes are corrected, it is without embarrassing or humiliating the students.

Creation of a positive learning environment is accomplished through both the design of the instruction and the training of the instructors. Careful design of the instruction around skills to be learned, rather than around time periods, divides the instruction into manageable bites. So, students do not have to work for long periods without receiving feedback for their efforts and experiencing a sense of accomplishment.

Instructors who are trained to recognize desired performance when they see it are able to respond positively to student progress.

12. Within the limits imposed by content and equipment constraints, learners are free to sequence their own instruction.

Students' motivation is strengthened when they are allowed to study things that interest them, rather than what interests the instructors. Interest in a given topic changes with time, and trainees working at length on one topic may desire to switch to something else for change of pace; therefore, modern instruction encourages students to follow their interests, within the constraints imposed by the subject matter and equipment. Limitations are placed on sequencing freedom when one skill must be learned before another, or when equipment is in short supply.

Implementation of this characteristic requires that students be fully informed about the sequencing freedoms available to them and the constraints that are imposed. By using a course map it is easy to show students the prerequisite relationships among the instructional units. In addition, the course rule, "Feel free to work on any unit for which you have mastered all the prerequisites" is used.

13. The learning environment contains the facilities and equipment needed to implement the above characteristics.

Since instruction occurs *somewhere*, though not necessarily in a classroom, it is possible for that somewhere to assist or impede the learning process. Care is taken that the environment allows implementation of the state-of-the-art characteristics described above, and that it does not provide obstacles to student progress.

Basically this is accomplished by clearing the environment of obstacles, such as distracting noise and activity, and improving working conditions by doing away with uncomfortable furniture and poor lighting. In addition, materials and equipment needed for learning and practice are positioned within easy reach.

GETTING THERE

Although there are other characteristics representative of instruction operating at the state of the art, those described above represent most, if not all, of the meat and potatoes. But knowing what meat and potatoes look like, though a starting point, is not the same as having some — just as knowing where you want to go instructionally is not the same as getting there. In the case of the instructional state of the art, getting there involves change not only for the instructional staff, but also for the students. For example, it usually takes two or three days for students to learn to become active in directing their own learning. However, with sound instructional design and strong management support, all the characteristics presented in this chapter can be implemented within a reasonable period of time.

SUMMARY

In short, state-of-the-art instruction derives its objectives from a real need (a job), creates instruction that is tightly related to the accomplishment of those objectives, and removes obstacles between the learners and the learning. It encourages and assists students to progress as rapidly as their growing competence will allow and makes their world a little brighter, rather than dimmer, when they demonstrate progress. It provides instruction and practice until each student can perform as desired, and then it stops.

A Model Course
(Tweakers in Action)

What would it look like all together? What would you see happening in a course that combined the best in troubleshooting strategy with the instructional state of the art? What, in other words, would a troubleshooting course look like when in "normal operaton"? To some degree, of course, what you would see would depend on the nature of the equipment being taught. There would be far more similarities than differences, though, because courses operating at or near the state of the art implement a common set of principles through very similar means.

What follows is a description of what one such course might look like. Let's assume that you and I work for a company that manufactures a series of complex equipment ranging in size from a breadbox to an elephant, and that we are scheduled for training in the troubleshooting and maintenance of one of them.

BEFORE THE COURSE

Approximately two weeks before leaving for the school, we each receive a short, course description booklet, giving us an overview of course goals and content and including a few photos of the course environment. We are alerted to the fact that our own competence will determine the rate of our progress through the course and that, while there is a maximum course length, the time we spend at it may be less than that maximum.

The booklet includes a clear description of course prerequisites and a short test to help us decide whether we need to brush up on anything before being qualified to attend. The booklet was routed to us through our immediate supervisor, who was encouraged to read and then administer the short pretest, a practice designed to minimize the number of unqualified people sent to the course.

Of special interest to us is the information about what to bring and about the amenities and recreational facilities available at or near to the training environment. Training managers know that, while these items are not directly related to school operation, they are important to the learners, especially if they will be away from home for more than a few days.

CHECKING IN

On arrival at the school we are pleasantly surprised to find that almost all the paperwork associated with registration, room assignment, and course scheduling has already been completed. After only a minute or two at the registration desk we are escorted to our room, handed a booklet describing school facilities, and allowed to unpack and settle in.

THE TRAINING ENVIRONMENT

On the way to our assigned classroom we look into a room where the course is already in progress and are immediately struck by the amount of intense activity. Everyone is busy. Some of the trainees are practicing adjustments or replacements on their machines, others are trying to locate practice faults inserted by their instructors or other students, a few are wearing headphones while watching a short videotape demonstration of a critical assembly procedure. In one corner an instructor is coaching two trainees through the troubleshooting of a common trouble. Everyone is engrossed, and when we walk through the open door of the room, nobody looks up. We then notice that the machines are bolted to the concrete floor, and that they are relatively close together. Later we learn that this has been done to approximate field conditions.

Upon arriving at our own classroom we are met by the instructors. They introduce themselves and show us around our working area: two rooms, one large and one small. A number of machines are mounted in the large room. The floor is carpeted in this case, not so much to hold the noise down but again to approximate field conditions. There are large pictorials on the walls, exploded views of assemblies and machine nomenclature. A poster labeled "The Ten Most . . ." lists the symptoms and troubles currently known to be the most common in the field.

Suddenly we're struck by a large bronze plaque with "Get It UP" emblazoned across the company logo. "What's that?" we ask.

"That's why we're here," replies an instructor. "The main reason for troubleshooting is to get the customers' equipment up and running just as fast as we can, and that plaque is a reminder to students *and* instructors that every activity is supposed to be directed toward that end."

He fumbles in his pocket and says, "I almost forgot. Here." He hands each of us what turns out to be a keychain with a small version of the same plaque. "You'll find that motto in a lot of places. Don't be surprised to find it on the tools we issue you. You'll even get a fancy version of it to stick on your toolkit when you complete half the modules you'll be studying, and you'll get a little something for your desk when you leave."

We slip our newly acquired treasure into our pockets.

"By the way, when an instructor gives you an UP thumb," continues the instructor while jerking this thumb toward the ceiling, "it means you're fussing with something irrelevant to the business of getting the machine up and running, and you'd better remind yourself why you're doing what you're doing."

He pauses a moment and smiles. "And if you get an UP thumb in the lounge or pub, somebody's telling you to knock off the BS and get to the point."

Along one wall a large cabinet contains spare parts, tools, and replacement chassis. Test equipment is mounted on sturdy rolling carts and there are adequate test leads, in good condition, mounted at their places of use. A large closet contains a variety of training aids, supplies, "bugs," and materials. In fact, everything needed for implementation of the course is readily at hand; nothing has to be signed out and transported from some remote storage location.

In the small room next to the equipment room, the instructors show us how to use a variety of instructional hardware: individual video playback machines, slide/cassette machines, audiotape players, and microcomputers for programmed practice of some of the troubleshooting skills. All cassettes, slide trays, videotapes and computer diskettes are clearly marked and are stored within reach of the machines they accompany. Even though the operation of each device is demonstrated to us, we note that operating instructions in large type have also been placed above each machine.

The few tables placed about the room are used for small group discussions called by either instructors or students or for studying materials that have to be spread out. We notice a television camera mounted on a tripod in one corner of the room with a portable recorder and TV monitor on a table beside it. "That," says an instructor, "is for taping practice sessions. When troubleshooting this equipment you will be talking directly to customers, and you will need to practice that interaction skill. Just as you need to be able to complete a service call without leaving crud all over the customer's floor, you need to be able to complete it without antagonizing or turning off the client. That videotaping equipment is there so that you can practice your machineside manner."

COURSE PROCEDURES

After being shown around the facilities we are invited to sit at one of the vacant tables, and one of the instructors explains course procedures.

"This is an open entry/exit course," he begins. "Because of the demand for large numbers of maintenance people for this equipment, the course is in continual operation. Trainees may begin on any Monday—the only reason we don't allow them to start on any other day of the week is that we are a little short on equipment—and they have up to four weeks to complete all their objectives. Four weeks is plenty of time, by the way. That will give you enough time to finish, with time left over to practice the things you feel weak in.

"You two are the only ones starting today." (That explains why we haven't seen other newcomers wandering around. We'd been wondering where they were hiding.) "I'll introduce you to the four who started last week. They'll help you get oriented, and they'll show you around the rest of the school."

The instructor then asks us to turn to the *Course Control Documents* booklet included in our materials and find our personal copy of the course map.

"This map shows you the entire course at a glance," he tells us. "Each of the circles represents one of the skills you will need to master before being considered competent to maintain this piece of equipment. Of course, you already have at least some of those skills, and the course is designed so that you don't have to study them again.

"The lines with arrows show that two modules — our word for lessons — are related and that the lower one on the map needs to be mastered before working on the one the arrow points to. But you can start by working in any of these three modules because none of them has any prerequisites and then work your way up the map from there."

"What if we already know how to do what one of these modules teaches?" we ask.

"Good question. When you read the objective of a module and feel that you can already perform as required, do two things. Skim though the module briefly just to make sure we aren't using any terms you aren't used to . . . we don't want to get in your way with words. Then turn to the back of the module and find the Self-Check. Follow the instructions — they're intended to help you decide if you are ready for the performance check. If you are, go over to that green box and take a copy of the criterion test for the module. Follow the test directions. If you need an instructor the directions will tell you. If you need a machine, you will be told on the test how to have it set up.

"An instructor will give you immediate feedback on your performance check. If you are OK, the master chart will be marked to show it, and you will be encouraged to move on to the next module. So you see, you don't have to study things you already know. You just have to demonstrate that fact to us and then move ahead. But when you run out of skill; that is, when you read an objective and don't feel confident that you can perform it right off, study the module.

"Though the modules are prepared as small booklets like this, they will direct you to explanations, demonstrations, and practice exercises on videotapes, slides, your lab machine, or whatever. Sometimes you will be directed to work with another student. In every case, however, you are free to move around as you need and want, and you are free to take your own breaks. Right at this minute I'm giving you what amounts to the only lecture of the course. From now on we'll be here to help, but you will direct your own learning activities."

"We both come from the same office," we reveal. "Can we work together on the modules? Sort of help each other?"

"Yes," answers the instructor. "You are encouraged to help each other practice and learn. But each of you will be expected to demonstrate your skills individually."

"What are the hours?" we ask.

"The rooms will be open, and the instructors available from 8:30 A.M. until 5:00 P.M., not counting the lunch hour. You are free to come and go as you please, but you are expected to be on time when a group or machine activity is scheduled. Other than that there is no such thing as late here. There is only performance."

We glance at each other with a look of disbelief. Who ever heard of a course where the instructors think of themselves as providing a service to the learners? And where learners are allowed to learn only what they need and at their own pace? But the instructor has been reading our minds.

"Please read through the other course procedures in the *Course Control Documents* booklet," he asks. "We actually follow these procedures, and if you run into an instance where we are doing something different from what the procedures say we are going to do, we want to know about it."

We read the course procedures. Everything seems clear.

"Are there any questions?"

"Well, yes. We noticed that out in the machine room there was one machine with a little red flag over it, and another one had a green flag. What is that all about?"

"The red flag means that whoever is working on that machine would like some assistance from an instructor. It's just a simple device to tell us where we are needed, and it saves student time . . . they don't have to stand there with their hands up. The green flag means that a performance check— criterion test—is in progress, and that whoever is working on that machine doesn't want to be interrupted."

"What do we do first?" we ask.

"There is a ten-minute orientation videotape that shows what this course looks like in action. It walks you through the whole procedure and shows you what you will be doing, how you will demonstrate your competence, where things are, and so on. It is a good place to begin."

"And then?" we prod.

"Then," says the instructor, "you can begin on any of the three modules at the bottom of the map. Read the objective first. If you think you can perform as described, glance through the module and perform the Self-Check at the end. If you can do it, go get the criterion test for that module and do what it says. It will have full instructions on how to proceed. If you want advice about what path of modules to follow, ask another student. Just remember, you are free to work on whichever modules you are qualified for ... that is, on any modules for which you have mastered the prerequisites."

Finally, we are told, "There are only three group sessions during this course. They are marked on your map. We have a sign-up sheet that will tell us when you are ready for it, and the module will tell you how to proceed. When you work on the TI module — that's the Tactful Interaction unit — you'll need to ask another student to help you with the practice part of it. Ask anyone. They will all be willing to participate. It gives them a brief change of pace and another chance to practice a very important skill.

"We're here to help you sharpen your competence. Call on us if you have questions, or if you just want to talk about something you are studying."

After the instructor leaves, we again review the course procedures and then view the orientation videotape. Returning to the table, we thumb through our course materials.

COURSE MATERIALS

Each of us has a small pile of material. We have already looked at the course map and course procedures in our *Course*

Control Documents. Riffling through that booklet again, we find a short glossary of terms and a Personal Progress Summary page on which we can keep track of our progress, noting the date on which we complete each of the modules.

There is a set of module booklets, one for each major topic. Each booklet contains one or more instructional modules. Looking through each module, we note the module objective on the first page. This objective tells us exactly what we will need to be able to do and how well. The test for the objective is also described, so we know in advance the circumstances under which that skill will be checked out.

Following the test description is a list of additional resources that relate to the module. Some modules list one or more videotapes, others list a slide/cassette program or a few pages in another book. We are free to use these, or not, as needed.

Next, each module shows us where its subject fits into the larger scheme of things, and why it is of importance. The module itself is fat or skinny, depending on the number and quality of existing resources. If there are many resources, the module orchestrates our use of them. If there are few or none, the module bears the burden of the instruction.

We note that each module also includes practice in the objective. Practice is always in doing whatever the module objective describes, whether that means working directly on the machine or working through programmed practice on the microcomputer.

Finally, each module includes the Self-Check, a simple tool to help us decide if we are ready to demonstrate our competence in the objective.

On further probing into our pile of materials, we find a complete set of equipment documentation — manuals, job aids, checklists, schematics, forms — that we will be using on the job. This is our personal set, and we remember that the instructor told us we will be using them constantly during the course, so that by the time we leave we will be able to quickly locate any information we might need.

We also find a page-sized card labeled "The Top Ten Troubles." This is a list of common troubles we will expect to find in the field given in approximate order of frequency, with the most common listed at the top. Since we will be working on a new machine in this course, we understand the list to be a best guess; it is compiled from trouble frequency information derived from previous machines of a similar type, from engineering data, and from the wisdom of the most experienced troubleshooters. We chuckle at the disclaimer printed at the bottom of the page, "Troubles subject to change without notice."

Finally, we discover a little plastic bag containing three special tools to be added to our toolbox. We will need them for making adjustments. Sure enough, "Get it UP" is molded into the handles.

THE COURSE BEGINS

Having viewed the orientation tape and pawed through our materials, we look over the course map more seriously. We select a module booklet to begin with and read the objectives of the modules it contains. "Hey," we say to each other, "it looks as though we can already do about a third of the things needed to handle this machine." It gives us a heady feeling to learn that we already have a leg up on the course, and that we won't have to spend time listening to lectures about things we already know.

We choose the module on operation to begin with. We are directed to a short videotape that shows us the operating procedures. It tells us that we troubleshooters will have to operate the machine well in order to do final tests, instruct operators, and check the results of trouble clearing attempts. Further, it reminds us that a significant percentage of the common troubles are put in by operators; therefore, we need to get into the habit of checking controls and verifying symptoms every time we make a trouble call.

After practicing for a while on a machine that has been assigned to us, we start giving each other troubleshooting practice. Nobody told us to, but we find ourselves inserting operator types of problems and then seeing how long it takes the other to clear them. This gives us more operating practice. We also enjoy a feeling of confidence when an instructor drops by and tells us, "You are already able to clear thirty percent of the troubles you will encounter in the field."

As we work we look around us to see what others are doing, and again we are struck by the fact that everyone is deeply involved in the activities of the course. Two trainees are watching a brief videotaped demonstration of an adjustment procedure, while another works through a slide/tape discussion of common troubles and how to handle them. Half a dozen more have their service manuals spread on the floor near their machines and are practicing making adjustments or replacements, or locating test points and taking readings with their test equipment. One trainee is sitting at the microcomputer, working through a teaching and practice program on waveform interpretation. Three instructors sitting together are intent on convincing each other that "Nobody Knows the Troubles I've Seen." Another instructor is watching a student green-flagging an adjustment procedure.

Though an uninformed outsider looking into these classrooms might think that all the different activities in progress mean chaos and no discipline, just the opposite is true. Students all know exactly where they are in the course and what they are trying to accomplish at each moment. Each is getting a critical skill molded into place before advancing to another, and every critical skill is practiced when it is first learned and then periodically reinforced throughout the course.

TESTING PROCEDURES

Every important competence is tested, not to pin labels (grades) on students, but to make sure that their skill meets the specifications described in the objective. Testing, therefore, is done for the same reason that waveforms or pressures are read: to collect information that will help determine what to do next. If students' skill meets the criteria, they are signed off and are free to advance to another skill. If not, corrective feedback is given by the instructor along with suggestions about what to do next.

Trainees are tested individually. If a module being tested involves troubleshooting, the instructor asks the trainee to step into the next room while a realistic bug is inserted into the machine. The instructor then calls the trainee back in and describes a symptom in the same way it is usually reported by a client in the field. When the trainee has located the problem and cleared it (if that is the object of the test), the instructor provides immediate feedback regarding the performance.

In every instance, the module test asks the trainee to do exactly what is called for by the module objective; instructors realize that to do otherwise would be like trying to measure voltage with a rubber ruler. Instructors are also careful not to fall into such teaching traps as using contrived or rarely found troubles or making trainees invent verbal narratives to "prove" that given troubles were actually the cause of the symptoms.

Although every test is realistic in that it demands the performance called for by the objective, not every test requires the use of the machine itself. Some ask for a demonstration of skill in the interpretation of test results, some for paperwork to be completed, one for information to be located in the documentation, another for a demonstration in instructing a pretend operator on how to avoid various common problems.

We notice that our instructors take every opportunity to remind us that troubleshooting is information collecting and not to ever feel ashamed or demeaned in collecting it from any available source. And then to make sure that we develop a strong habit of looking for the obvious before doing anything else, they periodically slip an operator-induced error into our troubleshooting practice and tests. By the time we are halfway through the course we ALWAYS check to see if the machine is plugged in, we ALWAYS operate the controls to confirm the symptoms we are given, and we ALWAYS try one or two rapid remedies before reaching for test equipment or diagrams. By then we've learned that there is big payoff in doing it like the pros.

We are expected to demonstrate our competence on each objective as we progress module by module through the course. We note that we are taking an average of one test a day. But sometimes there are none for two days and sometimes two or three on one day. We have noted that after the first day or so, however, we no longer think of these as tests. The instructors view these performance checks the same way they view a waveform or a pressure gauge, as sources of information about our progress and what we and they should do next to facilitate it. It's as though the instructors are on our side; *them and us against the objectives* rather than *them against us*. And we find ourselves looking forward to these chances to demonstrate our progress; they are opportunities to feel good about our efforts.

THE COURSE CONTINUES

Most of each day is spent actually working on the equipment, though we take whatever time we need or want to read, talk with other trainees, and work through instructional resources.

Instructors move from individual to individual or from group to group lending assistance wherever needed. We all feel comfortable about moving about freely, but avoid interrupting those who are in the middle of performance checks. We also schedule our own breaks, but we notice that an instructor will occasionally interrupt us with casual conversation if we have forgotten to pace our breaks as well as our learning. "Spaced practice is better than massed practice," they tell us, meaning that learning is better when done in short, frequent bursts of practice rather than in a long, grueling session. "Cramming doesn't work any better during the day than it does at night," they say.

Our evenings are largely free for relaxation, since we make good progress working just during the day. Even so, there is a lot of cross-talk about "The Trouble That Got Away" or "How to Spot That Elusive Trouble" or the best way to troubleshoot over the telephone. We aren't studying, but we learn a lot.

TOWARD THE END

When an instructor notes that we have only a few days to go before completing all the modules, he starts the outprocessing machinery; the registrar is notified of the probable date our room will be vacated, and airline reservations are made. Since reservations are made based on our self-estimated completion date, it is unlikely that they will have to be changed.

During the course, we have been asked to write our comments, complaints, or suggestions on a special *comments* pad located on a handy desk. Now we are handed a form asking us to provide feedback to help the instructors and the developers improve the course. Even though we have been making comments as they occurred to us, this form gives us a chance to carefully review the training program and to make suggestions based on our entire course experience.

We notice that this isn't the usual instructor evaluation form we have seen in the past. There are no questions about the theatrical abilities of instructors, such as whether they were interesting, held the chalk right, or used colorful slides. We answer questions designed to help the course providers spot unnecessary obstacles to learning; about which resources were useful and which were not, about physical arrangements and amenities, and about our thoughts for improvement.

There is another surprise. When we hand our completed feedback form to an instructor, we are handed a small package in return. On opening it we find a T-shirt printed with a large fist with upraised thumb, and the motto, "Get It UP," underneath. We suspect we will have no trouble remembering the larger purpose of troubleshooting.

AT THE END

After only two of the four allotted weeks, we have completed all the modules and have demonstrated our competence on each. We have learned to diagnose and clear the top ten troubles, and then some, and are confident that we can clear ninety-five percent of the troubles we will encounter. We know whom to call and what to do to handle that other five percent.

On leaving, we find that there is no end-of-course luncheon or dinner. How could there be, as there are people leaving almost every day? Instead, there is an informal ritual during a convenient part of the day when everyone gathers around while certificates of achievement are handed out, hands are shaken, and a small gold-plated pin shaped like a fist with upraised thumb is awarded to the newly competent. The ritual is brief, but the instructors enjoy it as it gives them yet another opportunity to make people feel good about their competence. It is another way to say, "Welcome to the club."

On leaving we reverse the registration process, pack our belongings and head for home. We are not given any job-related material on the last day; everything we will use on the job was issued when we arrived and was used constantly throughout the course.

ON THE JOB

When we return to our office we learn that our supervisor has received from the school a list of each of the skills we now have. This is more useful than a grade, as it provides our on-site trainer with information about how we can be helped further.

A couple of things then happen. We are assigned a territory and spend a week traveling with a more experienced TS as our on-site trainer, who teaches us procedures that are peculiar to the territory. And we are introduced to those one or two old hands to whom we should turn when we run into troubles we can't solve. The school wisely didn't try to teach us to solve every problem, only most of them—and *all* of the common ones—and instructed us to turn to the old hands when in need.

After a month on the job we receive a fat envelope from the school containing a questionnaire asking for the following information:

- Were we assigned immediately to the job for which we were trained? (Since skills can't be stockpiled like spare parts, this information will be used to determine whether other types of job aids are needed and whether there is a management problem in the field.)
- Do we feel that course attendance helped or hindered us in our job? (We are also asked to suggest ways we might have been helped to perform more competently during the first week on the job.)
- Do we actually use the test equipment listed and the various pieces of documentation and job aids?
- Have we developed job aids of our own that might be useful to others?
- Do we have further suggestions for course improvement?

At the same time, a questionnaire was sent to our immediate supervisor asking for this information:

- an evaluation of our proficiency when we began our assignment
- a description of our strengths and weaknesses
- an assessment of our progress
- suggestions for additional skills needed by those assigned to the target equipment.

LOOKING BACK

Looking back on our instruction, we find that it was all derived from the needs of the job itself, and that all course activities were directed toward sharpening our competence.

Although there were a few group activities and some practice with partners, instruction was self-paced, allowing us to progress as rapidly as our growing competence would allow. Sometimes we took more time on a topic than we really needed, but that was because we wanted extra practice, or it was a topic that particularly interested us, or it just felt good to do it a few more times before moving on. We had some freedom to determine the sequence of our instruction, and we had a great deal to say about the instructional resources we would use and the length of time we would work on a unit before offering to demonstrate our competence.

We found that all the tests were strictly related to the objectives, and that was a pleasant surprise. After attending any number of courses in which the tests included many items that were made arbitrarily confusing to "get a spread of scores on a curve" or that were unrelated to the thing being tested because the instructor liked to "vary the types of items to keep the test interesting," honest measurement was a welcome change. It was highly motivating as well. And it didn't make us waste our time and energy trying to psych out what the instructor meant. We always knew exactly what we would have to do to demonstrate our competence.

We were always given immediate feedback on our performance, too, along with suggestions for improvement. We were never put down or insulted or in any way demeaned. We were learners, and our errors were always corrected, but we were treated as equals by our instructors.

The instructors were great. Instead of acting like two-legged tape recorders, lecturing to all of us at the same time about the same thing, they served as consulting coaches, helping, advising, instructing, demonstrating . . . and visibly enjoying a good piece of work.

We were not required to learn the things we already knew, and when we were done, we were free to leave. It was terrific.

BEHIND THE SCENES

What we didn't see, of course, was the development of the instruction itself, the process that led to our being able to slide through the course unimpeded by the obstacles so common to other courses we have had.

We didn't see the analysts deriving the skills to be taught: interviewing engineers, operating prototypes, exploring blueprints, observing and interviewing experienced troubleshooters working on similar equipment.

We didn't see the designers drafting objectives and reviewing them with competent troubleshooters and then with management.

We didn't see the criterion tests and the modules being drafted and then tried out on a sample of prospective trainees (not colleagues of the designers) and then revised and tested again.

We didn't see the other instructional resources, the videotapes and the slide/cassettes, being drafted and then tested and revised.

We didn't see the training of the instructors that taught them how to operate a course in this learner-oriented manner, how to function as an ally rather than as an adversary, and how to facilitate rather than obstruct.

We didn't see management reviewing instructional policy to make sure it was consistent with the state of the instructional art and with the larger purpose of troubleshooting. And we didn't see management examining instructor review procedures, making sure that instructors are rewarded for following good, not poor, instructional practice.

There was a lot we didn't see because it all happened before we arrived. But the results of all that unseen preparation sure felt good.

PART 4

Troubleshooting Aids

Common Troubles

(The Dirty Dozen)

Given the tools developed earlier in this book and a picture of normal course operation, you are almost ready to troubleshoot your own troubleshooting course. All that remains are the facts about common course troubles—what they are, how to spot them, and what to do about them.

Typically being taught are errors in troubleshooting procedure, errors of content, skill practice, and instructional procedure. They represent practices that send troubleshooters to the job who

- are unable to locate an adequate percentage of troubles
- take too long to locate them
- cost too much to locate them ... in damaged equipment, unnecessary use of spares, or in alienation of customers.

Some of these errors will be within your power to correct; others will have to be brought to the attention of someone else with the authority to correct them. Some errors will impact on the time and cost of training; others will impact on the quality of job performance. All offer opportunities for improvement of the troubleshooting course.

WHERE THEY COME FROM

Instructional errors arise from a variety of sources, and a brief description of the main sources may provide some insights into better handling of the problems they cause.

Experts

By definition, an expert is someone highly competent in his or her chosen field, someone who does certain things better than most people. To become an expert, however, one has to learn to do those things so well that many steps are often performed "unconsciously," without thinking. It simply is not possible to become expert in anything if you always have to stop and think about each step, each action, and each move.

An underground gold mine manager, whom a colleague and I once observed, felt the wall and crumbled shale in his hand as he walked along the tunnel. He did this to determine where more shoring was needed but was unaware of doing so. When asked why he was doing it, he said, "Doing what?" When he was asked how he used shale crumbling to make his shoring decisions, he replied, "Experience." This is a common reply by experts who can't explain how or why they are doing something. The mine manager was undoubtedly telling the truth, but at the same time he was of no help in providing information that others might use in learning the same skill. Such people who are expert at their craft are often partially or totally unable to explain the components of that craft to someone else.

There's another point: Experts will sometimes provide wrong information about what people need to know or do in order to perform a job. This is either because courses they had included some irrelevant content that they unconsciously came to believe was important, or because the irrelevant content is dear to their hearts. Experts sometimes make a hobby of a subject that is irrelevant to the one they are teaching but allege that the hobby subject is important because they find it so personally interesting.

Lack of Instructor Training

Being a good troubleshooter doesn't guarantee an ability to teach troubleshooting to someone else. An ability to do something well isn't at all the same as knowing how to teach that doing to others. So, you can appreciate the problems that may arise when the faculty for a new troubleshooting course is selected. Often the scenario goes like this.

"We're going to need some good instructors to teach the new line of products. What should we do?"

"Let's assign our best troubleshooters from the field. That way we'll be sure to get the best trainers and the best training."

And so the experts are pulled in from the field and put into the classroom to teach the new equipment. They may or may not have the talent, inclination, or patience to teach. No matter. They are good at their job; therefore, it is erroneously assumed they will be good at teaching. What about giving them some training in the craft of instruction? The what? No, don't bother. "We wouldn't have assigned them as instructors if we didn't think they knew their job." And so they are put into the classroom with little or no training in the craft of instruction, an unfair practice for all concerned. When they do get training, it is usually on how to lecture . . . and this platform instruction is seldom seen in a course that is functioning at the state of the art.

In the absence of training, the new instructors have to do the best they can with what they've got. They're smart, they're dedicated, and they want to do a good job. That's a lot. But they can't implement a course at the state of the art without the requisite implementation skills.

It is very desirable to have experienced troubleshooters in the classroom, provided that they

- are given adequate instructor training
- prefer to coach learners to competence rather than perform at them.

Management Oversight

What happens when the precise purpose of the troubleshooting course hasn't been communicated by management to the instructional staff? There is obvious lack of agreement among those involved with the instruction about what the purpose of the course is. Will it be that of teaching trainees to solve every conceivable problem they may encounter, or rather to teach them to clear the common troubles as rapidly as possible? Or is the purpose something else?

In the absence of an understanding of purpose, there will be tugging and pulling among the staff about what should be taught and what should be emphasized. Some instructors will believe that teaching large amounts of theory prepares trainees to solve those rare troubles. Others will want to provide trainees with lots of practice in circuit tracing—or whatever.

Then something strange seems to happen to this staff when they walk into the classroom; it's almost as though they had entered another dimension. They seem to forget what they know about getting the equipment up and running in the shortest time possible, and that the trainees may already have some of the skills they will need on the job. They seem to forget the types of troubles that commonly occur or are likely to occur to the equipment they are teaching. And they begin to say things, such as:

"We need to teach these students how to think."

"Our job is to teach them to use the documentation."

"We're here to teach the theory of troubleshooting; the field teaches the practical stuff."

"We want to teach them to solve any problem they may encounter."

In short, the facts that:
- experts often have trouble remembering the step-by-step details of their expert performance

- experts may receive little or no training in the communication of their expertise
- The precise purpose of the instruction is not clearly communicated to instructional staff by management,

lead to a number of common errors in the teaching of troubleshooting.

WHAT THEY ARE

Here are the Dirty Dozen.

1. Not Teaching Common Troubles

Trainees are not told what the common troubles are or are expected to be (for new equipment). They are not given enough practice in locating and clearing these problems to easily handle common symptoms. They leave the instruction without knowing how to quickly locate and clear those troubles that account for seventy to eighty-five percent of the trouble calls.

This problem is easy to spot. There is no list of common troubles, either on the classroom wall or in the hands of the instructors. Students do not receive practice in troubleshooting the troubles associated with the most common symptoms, and instructors can be heard to talk about the value of "systematic" or "analytical" troubleshooting. They act as if it is demeaning for them to simply tell people what the common troubles are and how to handle them. When you ask them for a list of common troubles, they have several excuses for not being able to comply: "We teach students how to think" is one; "This is a new piece of equipment and nobody knows what the troubles will be" is another; "Students will have to be able to think their way through any problem that comes along" is a third.

The cure, of course, is to install a policy guaranteeing that all trainees will leave the course able to quickly locate and repair the common troubles. For existing equipment the list of common troubles can be derived from the experience of the troubleshooters in the field and the trouble frequency information stored in one of the company computers. For new equipment the list can be derived from

- troubleshooters experienced with similar equipment (at the very least they will know whether most of the troubles are likely to be electrical, mechanical, or hydraulic)
- guesses based on the most frequent customer complaints about existing equipment
- the experience of engineers and quality control people.

2. Irrelevant Content

Often when objectives are not carefully derived from the job itself, extra content creeps into a course, and more is often added as the course ripens with age. Although extra content may not have an adverse effect on course graduates, it will obviously bloat the time and cost of instruction.

Not long ago an associate and I reviewed a two-week course designed to teach customers to operate a computer. The entire first week was devoted to theory; so that the customers didn't get their hands on the product until the course was half over. This error is serious for two reasons: It bloated the length of the course and hence the cost, and it frustrated the customers. Though the instructors said, "The customers want to know the theory," the customers said just the opposite. "We learned a lot of stuff we didn't need to know, and we didn't get the practice we thought we paid for" was their reaction.

The question to be answered here is "How much course content is included only because it pleases the instructor, or because it has always been included?" To answer this you would use the list of skills (key skills derived from the job) that you developed earlier and your skill hierarchy (key skills and their prerequisite skills). Check the match between the skills that need to be learned and the course materials. Each item of course material (content) and practice should be keyed to the objective (skill) it is supposed to support. If the course developers haven't keyed the content to the objectives to be learned, you will have to try to do it yourself. When you encounter content that doesn't seem to be needed or useful for facilitating development of one of the skills, check it against your hierarchy. Perhaps that content is needed to help teach a skill that is prerequisite to one on your skill list. If not, it is irrelevant, and its deletion represents an opportunity for improvement.

3. Missing Content

It is also likely that there will be no instruction in one or more of the skills needed by the competent troubleshooter. For example, there may be an absence of operator training — instruction and practice in "driving" the equipment like an operator drives it. This omission is likely to occur either when the system is relatively complex or sophisticated, or when troubleshooting practice has been designed with undue emphasis on flow or signal tracing instead of focusing on information collecting from all available sources.

Similarly, there is likely to be an absence of practice in tactful interaction with customers. This is not a problem if graduates will not interact with customers. But when troubleshooters must talk to operators and/or instruct them, lack of interaction practice is a serious risk to customer good will.

Spot this problem by comparing the content of the course to your list of skills and look for mismatches. The cure is to bring the mismatch to the attention of those in charge and to explain, using your troubleshooting flowchart, the significance of the missing content.

4. Irrelevant Test Items

Troubleshooters have monotonous habits when it comes to measuring. They always use some sort of voltmeter when they want to measure voltage. Always. They never use a thermometer or a ruler or even a barometer … just to keep their measurements interesting. When they want to measure waveforms they use an oscilloscope. They don't use a scale or a torque wrench or even a pressure gauge. Boring. (Is he pulling our chain?)

Instructors often handle things differently. They use test items that have little or nothing to do with the things being tested, to "make my tests interesting" or to "find out if the students were paying attention." Don't blame the instructors for this form of instructional amateurism. Instructional tradition has until recently told us that is was acceptable to use measuring instruments that couldn't possibly measure the things being measured; that it was all right to use multiple-choice or true-false items to measure an ability to troubleshoot or repair . . . that it was OK to teach one thing and then test for something else.

This is an extremely common trouble. It pervades almost all instruction everywhere. You spot it by comparing the test items to the objectives being tested.[1] That is, you look at the skill to be learned and the measuring instrument designed to test whether it has been learned. If the test items don't ask the student to do exactly what the objectives say they are supposed to be able to do, the measuring instrument is incorrect. If the measuring instruments don't match the things being measured, there is no way to know whether and when the students reach competence. And you have found another sizable opportunity for course improvement.

Here's an example. Suppose that students are expected to be able to do the following.

> Objective: *Using the tools of the TS Toolkit, be able to adjust the framble frigits to the tolerance specified on page 35 of the* Magnificent Maintenance Manual *by Murky Mudge.*

---

[1] To help you learn how to match test items to objectives you might work your way through R. F. Mager, *Measuring Instructional Intent* (Belmont, Calif.: Pitman Learning, Inc., 1973). Shouldn't take more than an hour or so.

Then suppose that when the time comes for you to demonstrate your skill you are handed a test that includes the following item.

Describe the procedure to be used when adjusting the framble frigits.

Would that item be appropriate for testing accomplishment of the objective? Absolutely not! The key word in the objective is adjust. That's what it expects someone to be able to do. Can you find out whether someone can adjust by asking them to describe? No way. That's like trying to find out whether someone can play the flute by asking for a description of finger placement.

Some will argue that you can't adjust if you don't know the procedure for adjusting. True, true. But irrelevant to the point. The point is that you can't find out if someone can adjust by asking for descriptions of adjustments.

This trouble, mismatch between the measuring instrument and the thing to be measured, must be avoided if you want to find out how well students can do the things they are supposed to be able to do.

5. Theory in Blocks

Use of the word *theory* in relation to troubleshooting instruction causes instructors and developers to fall into a number of teaching traps, one of which is to bunch everything that is referred to as theory into a theory block. Students are then required to study the block of theory before they are allowed to see and handle the key equipment of the course. Another trap proposes bunching theory instruction into the mornings, thereby further restricting student use of the always somewhat limited supply of time and equipment available for practice. A third trap results from the allegation that to learn theory is the best way to learn to troubleshoot any problem that might arise.

The problem is not with theory but with use of the word itself; most troubleshooting courses do not teach anything that is purely theoretical. They teach people how things work but call it theory. They teach people that "when switch *A* is closed, current flows to point *B* and light *C* comes on," and call that theory, when what they are teaching is how it works. This confusion leads to endless arguments about how much theory should be taught versus how much practice should be given — a totally irrelevant question. The only important question to be answered here is "What needs to be taught to facilitate the development of competence?" What matters is that students learn what they need to know in order to get the job done.

Part of the problem can be illustrated by this example. Suppose that before you were allowed to practice taking someone's temperature, you were required to complete an entire unit in anatomy because "someday you might need to know about other parts of the body." Inefficient and frustrating to say the least. If you *will* need to know about other parts of the body, the time to learn about them is just before you practice doing something with them. *The point is not that anyone should teach less about how things work, but that they should teach it when that information is going to be used.*

The way to spot this theory-in-blocks error is to check the activities of the students. If they are spending their mornings, or any other block of time, studying things they are not immediately going to practice, you have located a sequencing error. Usually this error will not exist if students are using a course map as a guide to the sequencing of their work.

The remedy for this problem is to design each instructional unit around everything learners need to know to perform a particular adjustment, assembly, or disassembly; or how to use a piece of test equipment. That means that each instructional unit is likely to have some "how it works" in it — some more and some less. But there will be no large chunk of time devoted to overviews, theory, or fundamentals. A good practice is to discourage instructors from using the word *theory* in referring to what they teach. It will help them avoid these problems.

6. Disproportionate Practice

Several common problems are associated with practice. One has to do with the proportion of the troubleshooting practice allotted to the various course subsections or subsystems. For example, it is not uncommon for a troubleshooting course to devote most of the practice to electrical problems, even though most of the problems in the field are mechanical. Electrical problems are easier to simulate, less likely to damage the machine, and they provide instructors with "evidence" that they are teaching people how to "think."

Such disproportionate practice develops troubleshooters who are unable to handle common problems in the field because they have never practiced them at school. People who have not had practice troubleshooting mechanical troubles (or any other types of troubles) will be more hesitant in dealing with them and less likely to solve them than those who have had practice. No matter what the excuse, it hardly justifies sending graduates back to their jobs without adequate practice in handling the day-to-day tasks that will result in a minimum of down time for the customers.

The remedy is to adjust the proportions of practice time to more closely approximate the proportions of troubles seen in the field. This is easier said than done, however, because of rationalizations offered by instructors to preserve the status quo. One helpful tactic is to keep reminding them that trouble *locating* is not the same as trouble *clearing*. With that difference clearly in mind, they may be more likely to organize practice in critical adjustments and assembly/disassembly on normally operating equipment. It is not necessary to simulate a mechanical trouble in order to give people practice in mechanical adjustments, or to give them practice in removing and replacing those components or assemblies that are likely to fail. Similarly, it is not necessary to have to *remove* a trouble while practicing *locating* that trouble, nor is it always necessary to insert a mechanical trouble that might cause damage to the machine in order to give students practice in locating such faults. It is good training practice to describe or show students symptoms and then give them practice in associating symptom patterns with their probable causes. This exercise can be done in the absence of the machine itself and would be a good use for the microcomputer.

A similarity exists in the training of physicians who have to be able to diagnose (troubleshoot) and treat (repair) a variety of medical problems. Because diagnosis is important and quite different from treatment, several computer programs have been created to provide practice in diagnosis itself. The trainee, provided with one or more symptoms, asks the computer to carry out the tests a physician would order and report the results on the screen. The program instructs the student along the way in an attempt to shape up the efficiency of the information-collecting procedure being used. If, for example, the student calls for tests at random, not knowing what to do next, the computer might caution, "Doctor, you don't appear to have the patient's pocketbook in mind." With this procedure the learners receive a great deal of practice in diagnosis ... without damaging any patients. Precisely the same is possible for troubleshooting practice.

7. Unrealistic Practice

Related to the problem of disproportionate practice is unrealistic practice, which usually takes the form of bugs that are obviously faked or totally unlikely to ever occur. To simulate such phony troubles, instructors will often remove components, tape contacts, pack valves, or scramble wires. In addition, since many of these phony bugs are visibly artificial to the learners, the instructors might try to compensate for their artificiality. If a student points and says, "There's the trouble, right there. You switched those two circuit boards," an instructor might reply, "Prove it," in an attempt to verify the steps of the "reasoning" that led the learner to point to the obvious. If the learner cannot retrace the steps in a "logical manner" (which may be pure fiction), no credit is given for locating the bug.

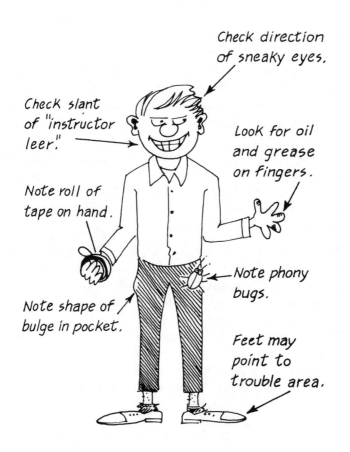

Instructors can rationalize all they want that phony bugs provide the desired symptoms; nonetheless, trainees see them as phony and the training distortion grows. Trainees exchange information about bug type and location with their classmates (this is not cheating because they are merely responding to the artificial requirement to outguess the instructor) and use detectivelike ploys to discover the phony bug before entering the room for their performance check. For example, they may look at the amount of time the instructor takes to insert a bug for a clue to its location and type. They may align screw slots so they can tell which have been moved. They may watch to see if the instructor has a roll of tape in hand—another clue to the type of bug that has been inserted.*

This is all very counterproductive teaching practice. For one thing, learners are asked to participate in a fiction, pretending not to see the obvious while going through the motions of locating the already located. For another, when they are asked to verbalize the reasoning process they allegedly used, they have to imagine the process they might have used had the trouble not been obvious.

Undesirable consequences follow.

- Though instructors say it is important to learn to be observant, in practice these instructors ask learners not to be observant when attacking phony troubles.
- Though instructors say it is important to learn to locate troubles, the consequence of doing so is mild punishment for the learner who is required to fabricate a story to explain the success.
- Time is wasted in psyching out the instructor and in observing his or her sneaky behavior, rather than productively spent in troubleshooting a real problem.
- New graduates on the job require more time to learn what they should have learned at school. Fewer trouble calls can be handled and those that are, take longer to complete.

---

*This procedure might be called troubleshooting the instructor.

A solution is to insure that instructors recognize the difference between trouble locating and trouble clearing and provide *realistic* practice in each. In addition, it is useful for instructors to take time to construct bugs that are as realistic as possible, such as specially created components that will show the desired symptoms in ways they would really occur. Instructors should also be prevented from requiring students to practice locating troubles that are highly unlikely to occur.

8. Backward Practice

A more subtle error is backward practice, a result of well-intentioned efforts by instructors who are competent troubleshooters untrained in the craft of instruction. It happens this way: Knowing that skills improve with practice, the instructors try to maximize the amount of troubleshooting practice they provide. So when they are locked into a lecture-in-the-morning, lab-in-the-afternoon format, they decide to use the classroom time to accomplish this goal. "How can I provide troubleshooting practice in the classroom?" they ask themselves and come up with an exercise something like this.

"Get out your schematics and turn to page 23-10. Got it? OK. Now locate resistor R-12. Everybody got it? Now then suppose that resistor was shorted to ground. How do you suppose that would show up?"

The students are then expected to trace through their diagrams to divine the symptoms that might appear if the selected trouble was present. That is, they are shown a trouble and asked to divine the symptoms, a practice that is exactly backward from what they will need to do on the job — look at symptoms and locate the trouble.

What's wrong with that? For one thing, it requires people to practice one thing and expects them then to be able to do something else ... a little like practicing a song backward in the hope that it will teach people to sing it forward. For another, it uses schematics as a bridge (crutch?) between the symptoms and the troubles. This suggests to students that

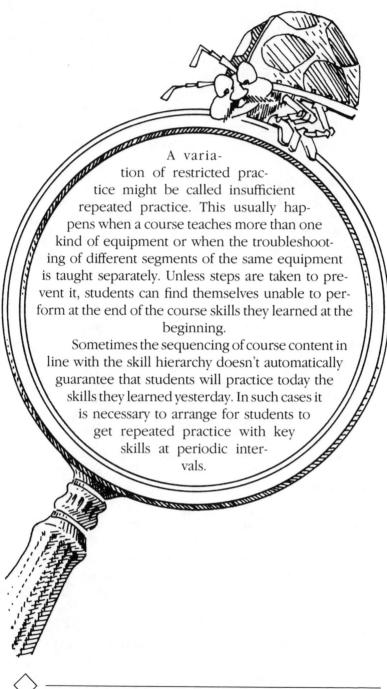

A variation of restricted practice might be called insufficient repeated practice. This usually happens when a course teaches more than one kind of equipment or when the troubleshooting of different segments of the same equipment is taught separately. Unless steps are taken to prevent it, students can find themselves unable to perform at the end of the course skills they learned at the beginning.

Sometimes the sequencing of course content in line with the skill hierarchy doesn't automatically guarantee that students will practice today the skills they learned yesterday. In such cases it is necessary to arrange for students to get repeated practice with key skills at periodic intervals.

schematics are the place to look for troubles, and that troubleshooters should head for them as a first resort, before they have collected and verified symptoms, rather than as a last resort.

The backward practice problem tends to appear only in courses that require students to spend large blocks of time in a classroom (lecture/discussion) mode. You spot it by observing what the instructors ask the learners to do under the guise of troubleshooting practice. The remedy is to help instructors understand that backward signal tracing is a counterproductive procedure, even though well intentioned. Instructors should be encouraged to provide practice that approximates job conditions; that is, moves from symptoms to troubles rather than the other way around.

9. Restricted Practice

Troubleshooting is information collecting. And efficient troubleshooters collect information from the most to the least productive sources, starting with the operator and troubleshooting aids and working toward split-half analysis. But how do good troubleshooters get that way? How do they get good at using an efficient troubleshooting sequence? By practice, that's how.

Unfortunately, many courses do not provide the kind of practice that encourages new troubleshooters to use an efficient strategy—that strategy has to be learned on the job. Often, course practice involves only portions of the troubleshooting procedure and is limited to the machine itself as an information source; a student is given one or more symptoms and is then expected to go to the machine and hunt for the trouble by using test equipment and documentation (diagrams).

What's wrong with that? What's wrong is that people do the things they have practiced doing; so, when these trainees get to the field, they tend to confine their information collection to the machine itself. They tend not to talk to operators or check for other symptoms or try quick fixes. Like the ten-cent bumbler mentioned earlier, they want to take apart the motor without first questioning the most useful sources of information about where the trouble might be.

Restricted practice, then, is practice that does not include practice in the entire troubleshooting sequence, and it artificially lengthens the learning curve—the time needed on the job to learn efficient troubleshooting habits. To spot it just watch the practice sessions to see how symptoms are presented to the students, and what they are instructed to do. If they receive no practice troubleshooting the entire system, you know that their practice is restricted. And if there is practice troubleshooting the entire system, then watch to see if students are expected to practice the procedure depicted on your flowchart. If so, great. If not, you have found another opportunity for course improvement.

As a remedy, initiate practice in what might be called the *total trouble call*, involving students in all the components of a realistic call from receipt of the malfunction report to filling out the paperwork at the end. In addition, introduce a rule saying that whenever students are practicing troubleshooting the entire system, they can ask questions of the person conducting the practice (an instructor or another student) who will respond as a typical operator would.

10. No Practice

It is possible for learners to work their way through an entire troubleshooting course without ever having had an opportunity to practice troubleshooting. How could such a thing happen? Several ways.

When instructors either are or feel they are limited in the amount of practice equipment available to them, they may offer only backward practice (as described above) or allow one student to troubleshoot while others watch. These watchers may complete the entire course without ever practicing for themselves. There is nothing wrong with the practice of assigning two or more people to a single machine, as long as course procedures require each student to practice the skills being learned.

Another kind of no-practice situation arises when instructional equipment is in such disrepair that parts of it are constantly down. I have talked with a number of troubleshooting graduates who not only never had a chance to practice their troubleshooting skill on some subsystems, they never once saw them in working condition. They wouldn't know what those systems should look like when they are operating.

On the other hand, learners sometimes get troubleshooting practice on the subsystems but never on the entire equipment. Given a problem in the hydraulic system or the electrical system or the mechanical system, they have some idea of how to proceed. But give them a problem on the entire system and they are lost; as they have had no practice in troubleshooting the entire system by working with symptoms they will see or hear on the job.

To spot this problem it is only necessary to determine how learners spend their practice time. If the course is operated according to a course map derived from the job itself, the last module studied will be the one most likely to provide practice on the entire system. If a course map exists, this problem probably won't. The courses likely to contain this error don't use objectives derived from the job. Ask students how much time they spend troubleshooting the entire system, and ask them whether that practice begins with the presentation of a symptom as it would be presented to them in the field.

This problem is cured by setting aside time for troubleshooting of the entire system and by providing trouble-*locating* practice from typical symptoms.

Testing without Practice

Don't confuse practice with testing, though. A course that tests trainees over the entire system without first giving them practice with the entire system is guilty of expecting learners to be able to do things they haven't been taught to do. Such courses are guilty of teaching one thing and then testing for another. This instructional error is in almost as much need of correction as that of no practice at all.

Documentation without Practice

It is also common for courses to fail to give learners any practice in the use of the documentation (manuals, diagrams, forms) they will be expected to use on the job. Often, on the last day of the course, trainees will be handed a pile of material and told, "This is what you will use on the job," a very unrealistic expectation.*

There are two undesirable outcomes of the lack of practice with documentation. The first is that troubleshooters will look clumsy during the first few weeks while they learn to fill out forms and complete other paperwork associated with a trouble call.

The second is more serious. Because people tend to do the things they know how to do, they will tend NOT to use documentation that is unfamiliar to them. They will tend to be frustrated when they try to use it under the pressure of the job, and then they will avoid using it again. If manuals and diagrams are critical to successful troubleshooting, they should be as familiar to the hand as a screwdriver or a meter. Thus, documentation should be introduced early in the course and used constantly.

There is a good reason why constant practice with documentation is important; most documentation is simply not designed for easy use by troubleshooters. Much of it is awkwardly designed, information is difficult to locate, and possibly incomplete. When this is the case, it takes constant use of these references throughout the course to (a) be able to quickly locate information in them and to (b) become comfortable enough with them to make their use likely in the field.

---

*i.e., lotsa luck

This problem is easily spotted by determining when trainees are issued their documentation. It is solved by issuing materials at the beginning of the course and then by providing constant practice in their use. Rule: Never assume that people will be able to do things they haven't practiced doing.

11. Murky Materials

This common problem takes the form of instruction that doesn't match the learners. It may not be written to match the learners' reading, listening, or experience level; or it leaves out important bits of information; or it is confusing or irrelevant. Such obstacles increase learning time and often send people from the training program thinking they never quite understood what was happening. Worse, they severely restrict the range of trainees who can benefit from the course, because it can take more mental ability to understand poorly prepared materials than it does to understand the equipment being taught. Bright people can learn in the face of a wide variety of obstacles while we ordinary mortals can learn equally well only if those obstacles are removed.

One type of instructional material that can often be called *murky* is the video lesson. The main problem here is not that the content is hard to understand, but that it can be largely irrelevant. Therefore, it poses an obstacle to learning; it gets in the way of getting on.

Although video is a potent instructional medium for demonstrating difficult maneuvers, for showing hard-to-see operations, and for modeling desired performance, it is often misused. The video screen is made to serve as an electronic manure spreader. In one version of this, a camera is simply mounted in the classroom, and videotapes of the lectures are then presented to the students, "y' knows" and all. In another version "shows" are created whose length is dictated more by commercial television standards than instructional need. Titles roll over exciting music, dramatic sequences follow, and narrators lull with their velvet voices. It's all very show biz, but not very instructional, and students could move along more rapidly without these obstacles.

It is difficult just to look at instructional materials in print or on a screen and decide whether they are clear and complete from the learners' point of view. Therefore, the best way to spot the murky material problem is to (a) determine how the materials were prepared and to (b) talk to the students.

To determine whether your course materials were prepared for the typical students who attend your troubleshooting course, check with your course designers to find out if the materials were *tried out* by some of those students and then *revised* and retried as needed to rid them of obstacles and insure their completeness. If they haven't been tried out by a few appropriate learners and then revised to incorporate the results of the tryouts, it is almost certain that the materials will be murky and much less efficient than they might be.

Short of redesigning them, the remedy for murky materials is more of a temporary fix than a cure. When, as the course progresses, you verify with your students that a course component is causing the same confusion from student to student, you can prepare a short instructional band-aid to help shore up the faulty materials. Write a page, prepare a drawing or diagram, or whack together a three-minute videotape to demonstrate a procedure. Key that band-aid to the material it is supporting by marking or labeling the material so that learners will know the band-aid is available and where to find it. Then, call the problem to the attention of the course designers.

A word of caution: It is not a cure to use every problem with instructional materials as a reason for delivering a mini-lecture. A videotape, manual, or set of slides and audiocassette can consistently help you band-aid murky materials while your valuable time is best spent as a coach—consulting, solving individual problems, and rejoicing over progress.

12. Instructor-Oriented Instruction

The purpose of instruction is to facilitate the development of student competence; it is best accomplished when students spend most or all of their time in active learning and practice. *Doing* is the key to competence. In a troubleshooting course that is instructor oriented rather than learner oriented, the instructor will be active and the learners largely passive.

You are in the presence of instructor-oriented instruction when students are all sitting quietly in the classroom in rows, facing an active instructor. The students are all studying the same thing at the same time and will move to the next topic when the instructor decides they are to do so. The instructor makes most or all of the learning decisions and requires students to spend large amounts of time attending to what he or she is saying (as though telling is the same as teaching or listening the same as learning). The severe disadvantages of such an approach are that some students are required to spend far more time attending to things they already know, while others won't have enough time to study the things they need to learn, and all will have far less practice time on the equipment than they need.

The full cure is nothing short of a complete course redesign to a competency-based, self-paced format. That requires the course developers to prepare objectives describing the important outcomes to be achieved and performance checks (criterion tests) that match those objectives. It also requires them to develop instructional units that can be studied independently by individual learners and a course map to help the learners make good decisions about what to study and when. In short, the cure is to prepare a course that matches the characteristics described in Chapter 7 as closely as possible.

What if you can't arrange for a complete redesign? Take heart, there are still some things that you can do. The object of your activity will be to increase the amount of student practice time and decrease the amount of time students must function as a group, at either lectures or demonstrations. First, using your skills list and hierarchy as resources, draft objectives describing the skills the students must have to be considered competent. It doesn't matter whether these objectives follow anyone's format for a "good" objective; all that matters is that they are clear. You can make them clear by giving copies to a few students (not other instructors) and asking them what they think the objectives say. Revise on the basis of their comments. Give copies of the revised objectives to the students and they will have a basis for deciding what they have yet to learn to become competent.

Then put your lectures on videotape. Just set up a camera in the classroom and do your stuff. Of course that isn't the best way to reduce the amount of passive-learner time while increasing the amount of practice time, but it is somewhat better than nothing if students can fast forward over the parts they don't need. Make the tapes available to the students, well labeled as to content, to use when they need them. Individually.

Next build a course map that shows students what they can study, and when they are eligible for that study. Use your hierarchy as a guide as well as your knowledge and experience about what should be learned when. That is, without violating the relationships between skills shown on the hierarchy, arrange units of study on the map in prerequisite order from the bottom to the top. (You may wish to review the model course map on page 128.) Don't worry about getting the map just right the first time. Give each student a copy. *If you are willing to listen to the students, they will help you to fix it.*[2] (This is much like listening to an operator as a source of information about equipment problems.)

Finally, write down the rules by which you will operate the course (use the set of rules on page 130 as a guide). Try to institute this procedure: "Each student must demonstrate competence on one instructional unit before proceeding to another." In other words, see if you can put the course onto a competency-based footing. Of course, you won't have all the

---

[2]For assistance in learning how to develop the components of a criterion-referenced, self-paced course refer to R. F. Mager and P. Pipe, *Criterion-Referenced Instruction: Analysis, Design and Implementation* (Carefree, Arizona: Mager Associates, Inc.).

bits and pieces you need to implement a state-of-the-art program, but you should improve enough to significantly increase (at least double) the amount of practice time available to your students. And the more time you provide for relevant practice of the skills on your hierarchy, the closer you come to a fail-safe course that will send students away only when they can perform as desired. (This is not to suggest that you allow *infinite* time for practice, but you can increase practice time within the course length you now have.)

THE DIRTY DOZEN

Here is a summary of the common troubles described in this chapter.

1. *Not teaching common troubles* sends graduates to the job unable to quickly locate and clear the problems they will face every day.
2. *Irrelevant content* bloats both instruction time and cost.
3. *Missing content* sends graduates to the job without all the competence they need.
4. *Irrelevant test items* make it impossible to determine whether learners have developed the desired competence.
5. *Theory in blocks* causes flaws in instructional sequencing and develops bad troubleshooting habits by teaching students to run to their schematics as a first, rather than a later source of information.
6. *Disproportionate practice* sends graduates to the job more practiced in troubles that are less likely to occur and less practiced in those that are more likely to occur.
7. *Unrealistic practice* results in counterproductive, phony, troubleshooting practice in school and requires unnecessary job time to learn effective troubleshooting skills.
8. *Backward practice* sends graduates to the job with troubleshooting practice that does not approximate the job conditions.

9. *Restricted practice* sends graduates to the job with a limited troubleshooting approach that must be unlearned; it is caused by training that restricts their information collection to the machine itself.

10. *No practice* sends graduates to the field with very fragile troubleshooting skills that must be strengthened on the job at the expense of serving customers.

11. *Murky materials* consume more instruction time than needed and may send graduates to the job unsure if they fully understood what they were taught.

12. *Instructor-oriented instruction* places learning decisions with the instructor, requires all learners to study the same thing whether they know the material or not, and limits equipment practice time.

There are other errors, of course, but these are among those most commonly found in the troubleshooting course. If you can correct even a few of these, you are sure to improve the competence of the troubleshooters you send out into the wonderful world of hardware.

TROUBLES IN MAINTENANCE MANAGEMENT

In addition to the common troubles found in troubleshooting instruction, some troubles occur in the management of the maintenance operation itself. Although these troubles are not internal to the instruction, they do influence down time and the cost of maintenance. Here are some to look for.

1. Rusty Skills

Often a long time elapses between the development of the troubleshooting skill and the actual use of that skill on the job. Sometimes this lag is unavoidable; for example, when equipment fails only rarely. If new troubleshooters are assigned to maintain equipment that doesn't fail during their first year on the job, their troubleshooting skill will be rusty when they are finally called on to use it. You can't stockpile skills the way you stockpile parts; skills require maintenance as much as machines.

Sometimes, however, the troubleshooting skill becomes rusty because managers assign a new troubleshooter to other kinds of tasks during the first few months on the job. When that troubleshooter is finally called on to troubleshoot, the skill is rusty ... and the manager is likely to complain about poor training.

When skills are used rarely, for whatever reason, the remedy is to provide periodic practice and well-designed job aids.

2. Dense Documentation

Although there are excellent job aids to be found in the troubleshooting world, they are not abundant. Commonly troubleshooters are sent to the job with umpteen pounds of awkwardly sized tomes designed more for engineers than troubleshooters. It is hardly any wonder that these materials end up unloved and unused. The potential consequences of poorly designed aids are that (a) the average repair time increases, and (b) troubleshooters need more instruction than they otherwise might just to learn to use them.

To spot this problem, just ask troubleshooters what documentation they take with them on a trouble call, then look to see which ones are gathering dust on the shelf. You may discover that the troubleshooters don't even *have* some of the prescribed documentation ... and don't care.

3. Sparse Spares

Troubleshooters can take longer than necessary when they don't have the kind of spares they need to isolate problems in minimum time. Often they have spare components but not the units that would allow rapid swapping to narrow the search.

This situation might be due to the high cost of spares, of course, but it could also be caused by an incorrect policy decision.

To improve the allocation of spares, ask troubleshooters which ones and how many of each they need to do a fast job of maintenance. Also look in their spares kit. Experienced troubleshooters usually manage to scrounge the items they need for doing a good job. I recently traveled for a day with a copier salesman who had scrounged *seven whole machines*. "When a customer calls with a problem the maintenance staff can't handle immediately, I swap machines. It's called service," he said. Is it ever!

You could also look into the computer records of parts replaced to learn more about the ones in most demand. Be careful how much weight you put on this information, though, since data suggest that about forty percent of replaced parts come under the heading of "False Part Removal." Besides, you already know that some troubleshooters replace the things they have spares for, hoping to clear the trouble quickly.

4. Counterproductive Punishment

Accidental or deliberate punishment of people responsible for getting the system up may unnecessarily increase equipment down time. In one company, for example, upper management ordered that a PM be performed whenever a service call was made. When they discovered this was not happening, they accused the maintenance staff of not having the right attitude and being poorly motivated. But, as usual, their glib finger pointing was inaccurate. Actually, field managers were evaluating their staffs, in part, on the *length* of a service call. Therefore, those troubleshooters who took the extra minutes to do the desired PM were less likely to be highly rated, and thus less likely to receive raises and promotions. In effect, they were being punished for doing what they were supposed to do. Since people learn to avoid the things they are hit with, they did less and less instead of more and more PMs.

In other companies, policy requires that the on-site maintenance staff call a designated 800 number for assistance when they can't clear a trouble within a few minutes. Suppose, however, that the voice on the other end of the 800 number responds to a caller's report with, "Hey, you turkey. Why the heck did you do that?" Or suppose that a call to the corporate diagnostic center results in the center getting credit for the fix, rather than the person who was smart enough to make the call? Obviously, these forms of punishment result in fewer calls . . . and longer down time for the customer.

Spot counterproductive punishment by making a list of things that happen *to the troubleshooters* when they do what they are supposed to do; in other words, identify the consequences of desired performance. If there are consequences that make their world dimmer rather than brighter when they act to get the system up as fast as possible, you will have discovered another cause of increased down time. The fix is to eliminate such punishment of desired actions.

5. Decentralized Training

Instruction is often carried out at the operating unit (field office, branch office, local office) instead of, or in addition to, instruction conducted at a centralized school. This is done because it has been decided that decentralized training is less expensive, easier to manage, or for some other reason more desirable. After all, on-site training can be especially realistic—the real world is directly available to trainees. And experienced troubleshooters with current knowledge of field problems are around. Practice is highly realistic when trainees accompany the old hands on service calls, especially if they are allowed to do more than watch and fetch.

Even so, there are common troubles associated with on-site training in addition to those already described. In fact, these troubles are so common that when you have occasion to troubleshoot decentralized training, you are sure to find large opportunities for improvement. Here is what to look for.

A. Mismatched Materials

This problem is caused when course developers are expected to prepare instructional materials for use on-site while sitting in their cubicles at company headquarters. They are never allowed (they should be forced!) to visit the environment in which the instruction will be used, and so they never learn about the conditions they should consider in their course design. Even though they may develop their instruction from good analyses performed by others, it is unlikely they can shape the courses into usable form. As a result, once the courses are shipped out from headquarters, they end up gathering dust.

Material that is awkward to use is almost always the result when developers are deprived of firsthand experience with the user environment. To judge the seriousness of the problem, you need only do a cobweb count of the materials you find in field offices.

B. Mismatched Mission

The mission of the field manager is to keep customer equipment functioning. Every effort is bent in that direction, not only because that is the mission but because squeaky wheels (customers with sick equipment) get a lot of attention. Because there are always things that need to be done *right now*, training not only takes a back seat, it can be considered a darned nuisance . . . and be neglected.

Spot this problem by checking to see whether the prescribed training is carried out

- when it is supposed to be (rather than as catch-as-catch-can)
- for each trainee who needs it
- by a qualified trainer.

You can also check for this problem by reading over the form used for annual salary review of the manager. (Of course I know that troubleshooters don't usually have the clout for getting hold of this sort of thing; but you ought to know how to find it, even though you don't currently have the corporate muscle to fix the problem.) When you read over that form, it is unlikely you will find anything at all mentioned about a training responsibility. And if it's not there, you know that no part of the manager's raise or promotion is based on how well the training mission is carried out. Look. If someone tells you to do something and then ignores you when you do it, you will tend to stop doing it. Managers are like this, too, and maybe more so. They learn pretty fast what pays off, and when they learn there isn't any real payoff to *them* for training, they tend to let it slide.

C. Inconsistent Instructional Quality

It is much more difficult to maintain quality instruction at remote locations than at a central school. (This is not an argument in favor of centralized training; it is only pointing to a common trouble that needs constant attention.) Why so?

- Turnover of instructors is usually higher in the field.
- On-site instructors are less likely to have much sound instructor training. Managers who believe that troubleshooting competence is the same as teaching competence may fail to require their instructors to learn the instructional craft.
- Untrained instructors are likely to conclude that they know better than the developers how the instruction should go and may proceed to mangle a well-designed course.
- The instructional environment is likely to be far below normal, consisting of anything from a desk in a noisy room to an unheated shack along the riverbank.
- And then there are all those brush fires to put out. These often seem to require the personal attention of the instructor, who just happens to be a hotshot troubleshooter.
- Finally, there may be stretches of time during which there is no one at all assigned to the role of instructor, trained or otherwise.

Little wonder it is so difficult to maintain consistent high quality instruction at remote locations. It can be done, of course, but it requires careful attention and good management.

Our industrial world includes a sizable army of dedicated and competent troubleshooters; if that weren't true, all that equipment wouldn't continue to hum as long as it does. And when chosen to serve as instructors, those same troubleshooters bring that same high dedication to the instructional task. Providing them with the tools and skills of modern instruction will give them a fighting chance of doing as well for students as they do for equipment.

A Troubleshooting Checklist
(Sleuthing the Sleuths)

You should now be able to locate the more costly errors in your troubleshooting course. It would be unrealistic to expect to find all errors, of course, since at the very least that would require the interviewing of graduates and their supervisors, as well as a client or two. Unfortunately, that scope of activity is seldom allowed the troubleshooting instructor. No matter. Clear the troubles described in this book and you will deserve the biggest hero medal in town.

In troubleshooting your troubleshooting course, you will need to review course procedures and materials, course objectives and tests, and the list of common troubles. You will need to observe how students spend most of their time, and to observe troubleshooting practice and testing procedure.

Here is a list of questions to help you focus your observations. A *No* or *Partially* answer reveals an opportunity for improvement.

Troubleshooting Checklist

	Yes	No	Partially
I. Troubleshooting Procedure			
1. Is a list of common troubles made available to learners early in the course?			
2. Do trainees receive practice in locating and clearing the common troubles?			
3. Does that practice begin by presenting learners with symptoms that typically appear on the job?			
4. Do learners receive practice in interacting with operators (clients)?			
5. Are trainees required to practice trouble-shooting in approximately the sequence of steps shown on your flowchart?			
6. Do all instructors agree on the purpose of the troubleshooting course?			
7. Is that purpose communicated to the students?			
8. Is there evidence that management agrees with the purpose promoted by the instructors?			
9. Are instructor rewards (commendations, perks, raises, promotions) keyed to accomplishment of the troubleshooting purpose and good instructional practice?			

	Yes	No	Partially
II. Course Content			
1. Is instruction offered in each of the skills needed for competent troubleshooting?			
2. Is the instruction confined to only what is needed to teach the pertinent skills (i.e., includes no irrelevant content)?			
III. Course Materials			
1. Does each trainee have a copy of the course objectives?			
2. Were the objectives derived from the job (i.e., from the ideal troubleshooting strategy, from associated tasks, from competent performers)?			
3. Are the instructional materials all keyed to the objectives — so that learners know exactly which sections are relevant for each objective?			
4. Are the materials understandable to the trainees? (Ask them.)			
5. Are all instructional materials available in in the training environment?			
6. Do the materials advocate the trouble-shooting procedures shown on your flowchart?			

	Yes	No	Partially

IV. Course Procedures

	Yes	No	Partially
1. Does each trainee have a copy of the course procedures?			
2. Do trainees report that these procedures are actually followed?			
3. Do trainees have a course map or similar document showing all the skills involved in the course and the relationships among them?			
4. Do course procedures pose a minimum number of obstacles between learners and the learning?			
5. Are trainees free to move around the training environment (subject to safety restrictions)?			
6. Do trainees have immediate access to course components, such as texts, manuals, videotapes, test equipment, parts, diagrams?			
7. Is the environment free of avoidable distractions (noise, interruptions, discomfort, harsh or low lighting, uncomfortable temperatures)?			

V. Practice

	Yes	No	Partially
1. Does each learner practice each key skill?			

	Yes	No	Partially
2. Is immediate feedback available for practice exercises?			
3. Does each trainee practice troubleshooting the entire equipment or system?			
4. Does each trainee practice all the steps involved in completion of a trouble call or troubleshooting assignment?			
5. Do instructors insure that each trainee can still perform each important skill when the course ends?			

	Yes	No	Partially
VI. Instructors			
1. Have instructors had field experience?			
2. Have instructors had training in the craft of instruction (in implementing competency-based instruction)?			
3. Do instructors believe in the troubleshooting procedure on your flowchart?			
4. Do instructors model the performance they expect of their trainees (do they practice what they preach)?			
5. Do instructors behave positively toward students rather than belittle or insult them?			
6. Do instructors seem proud of their trainees' growing competence?			

	Yes	No	Partially
7. Do instructors make themselves available to assist individual trainees during the entire work period (session, day, etc.), rather than requiring students to be available as audiences to them?			

VII. Learners			
1. Are trainees allowed to study and practice only those skills in which they need improvement?			
2. Are learners allowed some choice in the sequencing of their study?			
3. Are learners allowed choice in the method of learning and in instructional materials they use?			
4. Are trainees allowed to practice a skill *until* they are competent?			
5. Do trainees receive individual assistance when they need it?			
6. Are learners encouraged to demonstrate their competence (take the criterion test for the unit they are studying) when they feel ready to do so?			
7. Are learners encouraged to move to another unit of instruction when their competence has been demonstrated on the present one?			

	Yes	No	Partially
8. Does something desirable happen from the learners' point of view when they reach competence in all the objectives (favorable comments, cheers, diploma, time off, dinner)?			

	Yes	No	Partially
VIII. Tests			
1. Is every test item a proper instrument for measuring accomplishment of a course skill?			
2. Do learners receive immediate and constructive feedback on their test performance?			
3. When a trainee's performance is judged to be not competent, is the weakness diagnosed and additional assistance given . . . without belittling the trainee?			
4. Is the trainee required to demonstrate competence in each key skill before being considered a competent troubleshooter?			

PART 5

Spare Parts

The Victim Strikes Back

"All right, now," intoned the Chief of Clandestine Capers, "let's get this case put to bed. The victim was pretty badly pushed around and he deserves to have the perpetrators exposed."

"I dunno," challenged Snoop 8, "He asked for it, you know. Sucker for punishment, if you ask me."

"Well, no one is asking you," retorted the Chief, "and your dagger is making a bulge in your cloak. Now look, all of you, we were hired to do a job, so let's get on with it. If you've got some names, let's get them up on the board so we can see how many suspects we've got to deal with."

"I've got a name," offered a snoop. "It's David Cram."

"Again?" aghasted the group. "Every time we get called in on this job, there he is again. What'd he do this time?"

"Same thing. Tested the continuity of the manuscript in its earliest stage. You know, checked to make sure all the pieces were there and that the flow was close to right. Also provided a lot of moral support."

"He'll get HIS," chorused the group.

"We got the goods on another pair," offered Snoop 6. "Names of William B. Valen and Paul Whitmore. Also did a lot of work at the front end. Had to listen to the victim struggle through verbal descriptions of the content even before it was written, made suggestions, and even helped with the literature search. Furthermore, Ollie Holt also served as patient sounding board, you know, haranguee."

"Well," said the Chief, "retribution will strike. Any more names?"

"A bunch," offered another. "Nailed every one of 'em giving the manuscript a merciless going over. They wrote all over it and then called, wrote, or visited to make sure the poor victim knew what needed fixing. And every one of these suspects is a hotshot troubleshooter of large or small equipment, every one a heavyweight whose words scored big."

"Who ARE they?" clamored the sleuths.

"The very ones who verified the technical accuracy of the troubleshooting portion of the manuscript. There is Jack E. Vaughn, Sr., Herb Kneiss, William Holman, Carl Winkelbauer, Ernie Fiedler, Clair Miller, Lyle Reiber, Albro Wilson, Joe Bailey, Sharon Miller, Dell Coy, and several others who were observed in action or interviewed on the fly."

"Astounding," incredulated the Chief. "They will certainly be marked for their deeds. Is that the lot?"

"Hevvins, no," chorused the sleuths, whooshing their cloaks about their shoulders. And another stood up to report.

"After the poor victim, reeling by now from the heavy blows, made all the changes and had the manuscript retyped ... again, he subjected it to yet another round of tryout."

"Amazing," said the Chief. "What happened then?"

"Then," continued the snoop, "a clump of suspects checked the instructional technology portion of the manuscript to make sure it represents the state of the art. They skewered the booboos and fingered the faux pas. They are Howard McFann, Paul Whitmore, Frank Hart, Eileen Mager, H. Walter Thorne, and William B. Valen."

"And that ain't all," intruded Snoop 3, waving a sheaf of secret papers on high. "Here's some names of people who checked the draft cover designs. Victim said he wasn't gonna work his tail off on the innards and then package it in a brown paper bag. Said he wanted to test covers same as he did the other stuff. And they did. They did."

"Names," shrieked the Insufferable Interrogator. "Names!"

"OK," sniveled the sleuth. "Here they are. Jane Kilkenny, Gerald Anderson, Paul Attaway, Barbara Bennett, Steven Straley, Mary Lynn Goldrick, Brad Mager, Bernadette Nelson, Sebastian Finocchiaro, Deborah Haman, Pam Krotz, and Bill Latham."

"A likely list of suspects, and they will certainly get THEIRS," intoned the Chief. "But surely there can't be more?"

"Yes, yes," chorused the group, clinking daggers to the beat.

"I've got a name that'll tweak yer ears. She typed, retyped, cut and pasted, all with pleasant disposition in the face of changes, changes, changes. Name of Jeanne Mager."

"And THAT," grandiosed the Chief, "is SOME list." They all turned to look at · · · The List.

"What are we gonna do with 'em," asked a sleuth. "Turn 'em over to the National Roster of Book Batterers?" At that very moment a bookcase creaked open and another cloak whooshed into the room, an arm waving a document in the air.

"Hold it," gasped the sleuth, "I found this document while hunting for more suspects. You really oughta wanna read it." The paper was unfolded, presented, and ceremoniously read · · · in unison. It said:

I hereby proclaim that each of the above-mentioned suspects is indeed guilty of the contributions described, and that in accordance with the power vested in me by · · · er · · · a · · · well, I hereby request that the names be forever emblazoned upon the public view, so that said public may forever sing their praise and stand in their awe.

Signed,
The grateful victim

And so it was.

Los Altos Hills, CA
1982